SUSSEX SEAMS

A COLLECTION OF TRAVEL WRITING

SUSSEX SEAMS

A COLLECTION OF
TRAVEL WRITING

EDITED BY PAUL FOSTER

Foreword by PATRICK GARLAND

Alan Sutton Publishing Limited

Chichester Institute of Higher Education

First published in the United Kingdom in 1996
Alan Sutton Publishing Ltd
Phoenix Mill · Far Thrupp · Stroud · Gloucestershire
in association with
Chichester Institute of Higher Education
Chichester · West Sussex

British Library Cataloguing in Publication Data

A catalogue record for this book is available from the British
Library

ISBN 0–7509–1191–3

Typeset in 11/13 Sabon.
Typesetting and origination by
Alan Sutton Publishing Limited.
Printed in Great Britain by
Hartnolls, Bodmin, Cornwall.

To

Julian, Philip and Margaret

who would have joined if they could

The best travel writing is the book that can be read 'with almost equal pleasure in the region described or seated a thousand miles away with no prospect of seeing the place other than in the mind's eye. . . . A book such as this is as much a guidebook to the mind of the writer as it is to any definite region of the earth'.

Virginia Woolf

CONTENTS

FOREWORD

A Sense of Direction

Somewhere in the middle of his narrative linking the late William Plomer, wild daffodils growing anonymously near Steyning, an inartistic couple called 'the Colemans', fly orchids and Oscar Wilde, Ted Walker comments: 'Travelling is a matter of history as well as geography.' It concerns other things as well, I hazard to guess. Sometimes it is a matter of imaginatively going elsewhere by staying resolutely at home. Was not Kafka's *Amerika* a voyage of the mind as improbable as Jules Verne's descent countless leagues beneath the sea? Can we be certain the greatest traveller of them all, namely Marco Polo, ever visited the remote places he claimed to have seen, or did he learn about the unknown cities and silk roads from loquacious travellers? Did Shakespeare personally take ship to Venice, and if he did – for he seems to have mastered the psychology of a city built on floating sands, and the insecurity of a mercantile society – how is it he failed to describe it? Why, in *As You Like It*, is the Forest of the Ardennes so clearly Warwickshire, with French names, and why are Dogberry and Verges so unsuitably set in Messina? If 'This is Illyria my lady', then where exactly is Illyria – and what could be more imaginatively located than 'A Ship at sea; afterwards an Uninhabited Island'? All pose something of the same question: once the location has been specifically stated, it still becomes necessary to find out where it is. In his opening essay, on two Sussex churches, Tim Chilcott correctly sets the theme of this absorbing collection: 'There are places which settle with absolute precision and fullness', others that 'murmur about the edges of things, disturbances that undermine'.

Two features unite carefully, I believe, an intensely individual, sometimes idiosyncratic sequence of perspectives on one of England's ancient counties. (Are not all England's counties 'ancient'? No, Surrey is not, nor is Middlesex, without disrespect to those counties, for I mean it in Kipling's sense, the sense of 'Here the Romans halted' and that elusive atmosphere that perhaps they may also halt tomorrow.) One feature is remarkable enough – all our contributors are living, several are writers, many are scholars. Linked to the latter, a second distinction most noticeable within the pages of this collection, is the magisterial local knowledge of the area that so many of these writers reveal. Let us refer merely to a few of them, for to do otherwise, to be too sedulous, would diminish the surprise for the spontaneous reader, the dipper-in, the *habitué* of the bedside book.

John Wyatt's cheering evocation of Charlotte Smith (in which he salvages from the deposit libraries the best lines from the wreckage of an utterly vanished reputation) restores to us the late eighteenth-century bestselling poet and novelist. As much a survivor and as radical as Mrs Aphra Behn, who also wrote her way out of hardship and setback, Mrs Smith educated her children, delighted William Hayley – Blake's Hayley – before she seemed to have depressed him, and found, towards her life's end, a recollection in William Wordsworth's heart, while Dorothy darned a stocking, Mary baked pies, and Sara suffered from toothache. Vicki Feaver, an incomer to the county of recent vintage, with several poetry collections already accomplished, responds to the many inspirations near her home in West Ashling – the shallow mill-pond in her village, the horned poppy from the wild strand at the Witterings, and the bewitched yew forest of Kingley Vale, where, on a deserted winter walk, it is not hard to believe that the tormented shapes reflect the legendary transmogrificaton of sinister Danish kings.

There are other vignettes, drawn at random: Chichester Cathedral's spire – which crashed to the ground in powder in the middle of the last century, just at the moment a visiting child turned her head towards it from a railway carriage; Arundel – is it possible that its name is derived from the French for swallows, *hirondelles*? Ted Walker waiting for William

Plomer's train on Worthing Central station, and remembering that the Reverend Francis Kilvert (whose diaries Plomer edited and preserved for the nation) had waited there also. He knew Canon Andrew Young well, who told him about the Georgian poets, who in turn knew Swinburne. . . . And I recall Leslie Norris, at Bishop Otter College, where so many of us have both taught and studied, telling me that Andrew Young told him when he, himself, was a youngster just arrived in Sussex (which is the subject of his own contribution to this collection) about an old man who, when he was a young, curious naturalist, learnt all about the wild flowers and birds of the hedgerow from old, mad John Clare, in 1850, when he sat and chewed tobacco in the porch of Northampton church.

Leaps of memory take place here, even detective stories: is that elderly gentleman, standing between two rows of euonymus, truly the former companion of the famous Irish poet and playwright who in the 1890s came to Worthing? Did the medieval inhabitants of Hamsey share the saintly heroism of Eyam, in Derbyshire, and lock themselves away to face the rigours of the plague in isolation and terror, in order not to contaminate their neighbours? How can we know? The tradition is as tenuous as the sky, and the village long ago vanished as if its very existence was questionable. Or again, are there dragons and mythical snakes still to be woken in the lifeless black bottomless waters of the Knucker Hole? Certainly it is attested that an 'audacious large snake' terrified locals in 1867. If it could do so then, why does it not today? Lyall Watson is enthusiastically quoted: 'We need our dragons.'

Chanctonbury Ring is claimed to be the most haunted hilltop in Britain, and sailing the South Saxon shore uncovers below the southerly driven Spring tide, the often quoted myth of the bells of *la cathédrale engloutie* of St Wilfrid, built improbably upon Bognor Rocks. Centuries earlier, ruins were descried, at seabed floor, of Saxon villages around the perimeters of the Deer Park, clearly marked on my seventeenth-century map. Bognor has been such an unlikely magnet for the intelligentsia: James Joyce worked on papers of

Finnegans Wake in Clarence Road; Virginia Woolf, aged fifteen, stayed at 4, Cotswold Crescent in 'misty, muddy, flat, utterly stupid Bognor (the name suits it)'; George V abused it; but D.H. Lawrence, standing on the pier, had an apocalyptic vision of the ghost legions of Flanders dead marching out of the sea in 1915. One writer's ghastly monotone can be another's epiphany.

A symbol of the decline of pastoral England, the rural prosperity – and tranquillity – for Hilaire Belloc and an earlier generation, Ha'nacker Mill, may exist still, but by no means in desolation: 'Ha'nacker's down and England's done', declares Belloc, but the windmill (a detail in Stubbs' great portrait of the Charlton Hunt, still in Goodwood House) was carefully restored by the sixth Duke of Richmond and Gordon and Sir William Bird of Eartham, and is the object of a pilgrimage made by a father and daughter, also in quest of relics at nearby Boxgrove. Six-year-old Maisie, contemplating the infinite and the unknowable, queries the age of Boxgrove Man, a representative of European humanity's earliest inhabitants (conveniently domiciled in the local gravel – albeit no more than a few teeth and part of a lower leg bone) and ruminates to herself whether it is plausible that Boxgrove Man lives in Halnaker Mill!

But finally, after all this journeying, the editor himself calls a halt in his Sussex garden, burrowing his fingers in the October soil to tickle out potato tubers, as warm and fresh and round as hens' eggs. At journey's end, is it mistaken to remember the parallel delight of Richard Jefferies, poet of the South Downs' shepherds, when he picked up a piece of clod and crumbled it in his fingers: '. . . it was a joy to touch it – I held my hand so that I could see the sunlight gleam on the slightly soft surface of the skin. The earth and sun were like my flesh and blood, and the air of the sea, life.'

Patrick Garland

Acknowledgements

Books that are a collaborative venture rely very much on the good spirit and cooperation of everyone concerned. This has certainly been my experience, and I record here my warm appreciation:

to the writers, all of whom have contributed in one capacity or another to the teaching of English at the Chichester Institute of Higher Education, for, in many cases, the past decade and more;

to the many individuals who have helped the writers achieve their goal: their names are not entered here (there were too many), but the writers know to whom they are indebted and I ask that my appreciation is passed on too;

to Patrick Garland, who agreed not only to contribute a poem but also to write the foreword;

to John Davis, who permitted a detail from his painting of Ditchling Beacon to be used on the cover;

to Tony (and Jean) Barnes, whose camera has contributed so much to the whole volume;

to Jaqueline Mitchell and Clare Bishop, whose professional advice and guidance have been especially appreciated;

to Vivienne Frost, who tackled the needs of the publisher with effective efficiency and good humour;

to Susannah Foreman, who has shared the pleasure of completion;

and to Jane Hare, Shaun Payne and Lesley McCarthy, who each, unbeknown to the other, discovered that what is not marked on a map of Sussex is more beguiling than what is.

For financial support, I am pleased to acknowledge assistance from Stuart Dobbin (Finance Officer) and Dr T. Chilcott (Dean of Faculty, Arts and Humanities).

For permission to publish illustrations I extend grateful thanks to:

Revd Peter Smith and the Parochial Church Council at St Michael's, Berwick and Tim Chilcott, (p. 4); Tim Chilcott (p. 8); Bishop Otter Trustees (p. 28); Her Majesty's Stationery Office (p. 44); Hydrographic Office, Taunton (p. 52); John Davis (cover and pp. 57 and 116); Mary Evans Picture Library (p. 79); Imperial War Museum (p. 84); Tate Gallery Archive (pp. 89 and 91); J.T. Tupper, Bignor Roman Villa (p. 118); Tate Gallery Picture Library (p. 152); Tim McCann and the West Sussex Record Office (p. 159); Revd I. Rutherford and the Parochial Church Council, St Michael's, Paulsgrove (p. 167); J.A. Gowen and the Trustees of Stansted Park Foundation (p. 170); and to Tony Barnes for pp. 13, 21, 23, 37, 61, 65, 109, 119, 133, 139, 146, 148, 149, 154, 158, 175, 186.

Paul Foster
23 November 1995
Chichester Institute
of Higher Education

TWO CHURCHES IN SUSSEX: ST MICHAEL'S, BERWICK AND HAMSEY OLD CHURCH

Tim Chilcott

When I think about places, they often seem to be written on my mind in two quite different ways. There are those that settle with absolute precision and fullness. The exact wash of colour and light in that particular spot, on a building, a field, a sky; a single sound heard singly, or mingling with another in precisely that way; a texture or taste or smell experienced with just such a focus – these are places that inscribe themselves with complete authority. And the authority derives from much more than sensory awareness, however vividly remembered. Places like these evoke a sense of context and continuum. They announce themselves as an assurance, a knowledge, a confirmation. They have created their own meaning – and for the time that you are in them, and for ever after, they assert their identity as places. 'I am not an imagining,' they declare to those who visit them, 'not a fiction, not an interpretation. I am my own significance. I have located myself. I know why I am a place.'

There are other places, though, that have been written more indeterminately. The sensory focus is less secure. Were they seen in summer or autumn, morning or afternoon? Once or several times? Was it that sound that was heard or another, confused now from some other place? Why have the taste and smell been lost? And the uncertainty derives from more than the inevitable selections of memory. For even when you stand in such places, there is a strange absentness about them. You see them, hear them, are surrounded by them – but all that is marginal, because they are in fact elsewhere, shifting through different prisms of light, different chambers of sound. They murmur about the edges of things, fluctuations, disturbances that undermine. 'I do not know whether I am real or phantom,' they whisper, 'whether truth or merest dream. I seem to have lost location, the very thing that conferred identity.'

In East Sussex, there are two spots within ten miles of each other that evoke this contrast ever more powerfully with each return. Both are churches, and have stood on the same sites for more than a thousand years. Over the millennium, both have undergone comparable periods of neglect and rebuilding, restoration and decay, that is the fate of all but the most star-blessed places. Both, too, now survive in an eclectic mixture of architectural styles from Norman through Early English and Decorated to Perpendicular and later. But there the similarities begin to falter. In their interiors and exteriors, in the landscapes that surround them, they speak in different tongues. The two churches are St Michael and All Angels in Berwick, and Hamsey Old Church, just north of Lewes.

St Michael's is best approached from the height of the South Downs, a mile or so before the chalk escarpment falls down to the village of Alfriston and the Cuckmere River. From the crest of the Downs, some six hundred feet up at this point, the church appears in the middle of the fertile greensand plain below, part of a broad and generous pattern of farms and fields and settlements. Only as you draw nearer is it evident that, like all the churches along the line of Alciston, Lullington, Alfriston, Wilmington and Willingdon, it is built on slightly higher ground, almost certainly on a pre-Christian barrow. Closer to, you notice also that its spire, rising above the comforting enclosure of trees, is slightly out of true line, the result of the 1987 hurricane. This is a minor blemish, though, on a building that now belies the extensive reconstruction undertaken during the nineteenth century by its longest serving curate and rector, Edward Boys Ellman. The stone and flint and ancient timbers have composed themselves into a regularity, a kind of lucidity. As you draw near, you sense the steady rhythms of a rural community that has changed little across the draw of centuries. This is a proportionate place, following the patterns of the seasons in uninterrupted grace.

If you know nothing about St Michael's, the first view of the interior might for a moment disappoint. No streaming light through the glories of medieval stained glass, but plain unadorned windows. No cascades of sound from bells or organ, for only one bell remains and the organ is similarly restrained. All that can be seen, as the eyes adjust to the dimness, is that the walls are covered with indistinct colour and shapes. A sign invites you to turn on the lights – and as you do so, the entire building arcs into a shout of colour. Blues of gowns and uniforms and skies, greens and browns of hills and trees, whites of dresses and wings and lilies – scenes of the annunciation, Christ's nativity, the supper at Emmaus, Christ in glory, all set in a Sussex landscape of chalk pit and beacon, tended garden and rolling downland. In the chancel, over the arch, on the screen, on the north, south and west walls, on the pulpit panels – the interior is saturated with colour and form and plenitude. These are the murals painted on almost every vertical surface by Duncan Grant, Vanessa Bell and her son, Quentin, during the early years of the Second World War.

The major support for decorating the church in this way came from G.K.A. Bell, Bishop of Chichester from 1929 to 1957. In the conviction that contemporary art and artists must contribute towards the structure and adornment of churches, if such buildings were not to fossilize into dead records, he enlisted the support of the celebrated group who lived only two miles away in Charleston Farmhouse, under the crest of Firle Beacon. The murals were to be painted on plasterboard, so allowing the artists to work at Charleston, and only later to be fixed to the walls of the church. Maynard Keynes lent his barn as a studio; John Christie sent over some large-scale easels from the theatre at Glyndebourne; and after some local opposition had been overcome, work began in late autumn 1941. Towards the end of November, Vanessa Bell wrote to her daughter, Angelica: 'The house is chaotic, and all a dither with Christianity.' From the dither, a year later, the wall-paintings were completed and hung. They were dedicated by the bishop in October 1943.

If there is a single imaginative thread that draws together the details of this interior, it is the fusion of time and timelessness, the sense of a historical moment set in the greater continuum of seasonal growth and decay, and of Christian parable and belief. Many of the human figures seem almost to have been photographed, so immediate and exact is their attitude. Two local shepherds and their sons, as well as the artists' gardener and the son of their housekeeper, posed as models for Vanessa Bell's evocation of the nativity scene. Angelica Bell and a friend were similarly used in the painting of the annunciation. More moving, perhaps, the models for the two disciples at Emmaus were men of the Australian Air Force stationed in Sussex during the war; and one of the three representatives of the

Vanessa Bell's painting of the nativity: St Michael and All Angels, Berwick.

armed forces who kneel in a field of poppies and wild flowers to the left of the chancel arch – the soldier Douglas Hemming – was killed in the assault of Caen in 1944. To some, their positions may seem stiff, studied, even rhetorical. But these are not human figures abstracted or mythologized. They sustain their own reality, known through the domestic, local moments that are the stuff of every life. In the nativity scene, the manger is a Sussex barn at Tilton, the lamb the Southdown strain developed by Ellman of Glynde, the basket a Sussex trug. The shepherds carry Pyecombe crooks, and in the centre distance is Mount Caburn near Lewes. At the same time, details like these merge imperceptibly into the larger repeated patterns of time. Four roundels by Duncan Grant depict – in vibrant, Breughel-like colour – the seasons of the year; a further pair of paintings show the pond outside Charleston at dawn and at sunset. Another set of small panels by Quentin Bell evokes the cycle of human life, from baptism, through confirmation and repentance, to communion, marriage and finally the last rites. Everywhere, the local resonates with the universal, the specific observations of particular people and particular places with a larger timelessness. This is both Sussex and everywhere, both war-time England and every time. In words written within months, even days, of the wall-paintings, the root of the place is understood:

> You are not here to verify,
> Instruct yourself, or inform curiosity
> Or carry report. You are here to kneel
> Where prayer has been valid . . .
> Here, the intersection of the timeless moment
> Is England and nowhere. Never and always.

The epiphanies of T.S. Eliot's *Little Gidding*, when time intersects with timelessness, are echoed here, in St Michael and All Angels – confirming, placed within meaning.

Viewed from afar, from the four-hundred foot height of Offham Hill, Hamsey Old Church – like St Michael's, Berwick – stands out on a knoll, surrounded by flat agricultural land. Yet even at this distance the mound does not seem to integrate but to isolate. Encircled on three sides by an oxbow formed in the River Ouse, and on the fourth by a watercourse cut in the eighteenth century to make the river more navigable for barges, the area of the church is to all intents and purposes an island, marooned. There is only one approach, through a farmyard that seems perpetually muddy even in high summer, past rusting cowsheds and machinery, and up the one-track road. The west tower comes into view first, strong yet squat and unlovely. Near the top, a gargoyle, its mouth grotesquely agape in laughter or in pain, is rendered even more grotesque by having only one ear. The weather vane seems to have rusted fast. You come to the church door and find it locked. The key is reputed to be found somewhere in the cowshed, back in the farmyard.

The interior of Hamsey Old Church is in fact regularly seen only five Sundays during the summer months, when services are held. Inside, there could be few greater contrasts with the exuberance of St Michael's. Now, colour and fullness and marvel are replaced by spareness, age, austerity. The inner walls of the tower are pitted with put-log holes. There is no pulpit, no lectern, only a few pews, some of which are four hundred years old. In the chancel, a canopied tomb, known as the de Say or Founder's tomb, after Geoffrey de Say who was once thought to have built the church, contains in fact the remains of Edward Markwick, who died three centuries later in 1538. In his will he prescribed that 'an Image and Scripture should there be graven whereupon the Sepulchre may be sett'. But there is no image and no scripture. Both the top and the heraldic shields on the front are completely bare. The memorial bears a strange anonymity, almost a kind of dereliction.

It is as you stand at the church porch, however, and look out over the middle distance that the atmosphere of the place takes special hold. The land between the church and Offham Hill to the west, or Lewes to the south, has a curious absence about it, a sense of remoteness for all its geographical proximity. In the mid-nineteenth century, the feeling of inaccessibility was so strong that the then rector proposed the building of a new church in the parish, complaining that

> the present Church has long been found . . . to be totally inadequate to the spiritual wants of the parish. It is situated at its very extremity, far distant from the residences of the greater part of the population, and only to be approached by much exposed and very bad roads.
>
> The fatal consequences of this difficulty in reaching the Church during the greater part of the year is seen by the small proportion of the parishioners (chiefly men) who are able to attend it, and severely felt by the old and infirm who at no time are ever able to do so.

The new church was built, the old one abandoned, to the extent that a commentator in 1865 considered it 'so far dilapidated as to be unfit for worship'. Although now more cared for, the church continues to evoke a sense of bareness, of standing at the edge of things, away from human habitation. What in the mind's eye is lacking is the village that should surround it, the daily life of people going about their common rounds. This is place, not as fulfilment, but as deprivation.

In fact, there was once a village at Hamsey which has now disappeared. Deep in local tradition, there is a legend that continues to be told. It is that the villagers of Hamsey were at some time in the past visited by the plague. What form it took, and when, is unknown. It might have been any of the contagions that spread throughout England and Europe between the Black Death of the fourteenth century and the great plague of 1665. Of their fatal virulence, however, there can be no doubt. In nearby Michelham Priory, only five brothers out of thirteen survived the arrival of the Black Death in 1348–9. More than half the monks at Battle Abbey died. Three centuries later, between a quarter and half of local populations are thought to have perished. Perhaps with a knowledge of such fatality, one version of the tradition speaks of a special kind of selflessness. Recognizing that they had been

7

Hamsey Old Church, north of Lewes.

infected, the villagers of Hamsey refused all contact with the
outside world. In doing so, they ensured that the plague did
not spread. But whether any of this took place, and, if so, to
whom and to how many, is unrecorded. There is no tablet on
church wall or in the graveyard, no written account extant, not
a single stone in the surrounding land to indicate a village
might once have been here. Now, only the refractions of
imagination persist, the phantoms of the mind playing on a
space that is devoid and hidden.

Hamsey Old Church is doubtless seen most atmospherically
at twilight, under the growl of late November clouds,
darkening as they twist in the scud of wind. The bare trees on
the north-eastern side of the mound provide no screen from the
gusts racing across the water meadows of the Ouse. At such a

season and time of day, ghosts begin to walk. Pip is terrified by Magwitch, Heathcliff roams abroad, a thousand Gothic nightmares begin. But I have seen the church under even more compelling conditions: the stiff heat of a long summer's afternoon, when the sky was blue-white with dazzle, and the warmth flowed into every pore of the body. The place, I thought, should be changed in such weather and at such a season – should be eased into a similar, restoring warmth. But the church stood there on its mound, untransformed, resistant to the summer's heat, finding some final invulnerability in the sheet of haze. And then there came a memory that the plague had often been worst during the summer months, when heat intensified its infectiousness. And from somewhere inside the church, or from the soil beneath, there seemed to come another echo: the dissolving litanies of the Book of Common Prayer. 'From plague and pestilence and sudden death, good Lord, deliver us.' They might have intoned those words – the villagers in Hamsey church – trusting that this place's hallowedness would confer a meaning. But the place shifted away from their centre into another, which their language could not reach.

In my mind's eye, St Michael's, Berwick and Hamsey Old Church are emblems of a much larger space, a greater tension that pulses through the many contours of the land of Sussex. One pulse is nurturing, civilizing, mutual, speaking of place and home and human construction. 'I am peopled,' says the place; 'I have found a place,' say the people. The other pulse is raw, unyielding, pointing to the fragility of civilization's hold, the ease with which more silent, ancient drives might reassert themselves. Against the confirming domestic interior of St Michael's stands the world of barrow and plague, chalk pit and combe. And sometimes, high up on the Downs in a November twilight, there comes a sense that the chthonic pulse, more regular and ageless than the heart's beat, is only waiting till its time should come again.

DRAGONS IN OUR MIDST: BIGNOR HILL AND LYMINSTER POOL

Jessica De Mellow

We need our dragons. They remind us of our origins and our incompleteness.

(Lyall Watson)

Force your way across the traffic on the A27, turn past the drive-in MacDonald's, and you stand in dragon country. We wait transfixed, ankle deep in mud, watching large, green bubbles rise from the dark heart of the dragon's pool. Across fields of sour weeds a train clamours past, gushing smoke. Beyond six feet of barbed wire fencing, the water stirs again.

The green mild hills, woods and pools of West Sussex swarm with legends of dragons and mythical snakes. We spent a morning among volumes of local folklore, mapping each site with a dark pencil. The dragon trail begins in St Leonard's Wood near Horsham, where the sixth-century saint fought a ferocious battle with a scaled beast. It winds down to the serpent's nest of Cissbury Hill and the bottomless Knucker Hole of Lyminster, loops up and around Bignor Hill, and swallows its own tail near Fittleworth, where an 'audacious large snake' terrified locals in 1867. Within a rough circle of twenty miles, five dragons have guarded their treasure and dined on local people for almost two thousand years. Some of these legends are half-forgotten, superseded by contemporary bogeys of orange brick and industrial smoke; others, like the Lyminster dragon of the Knucker Pool, are more deliberately preserved. Childhood memories of dragon hunts rose rich as the smell of toffee as we studied our scribbled map in the fluorescent light of the library. Why West Sussex? And why *dragons*?

The dragon hunter hoping to find fabulously winged and fiery legends in the Sussex hills will be disappointed, for the British dragon is as phlegmatic as its native climate. More giant serpent or 'worm' than that fiery beast of the classical Greek imagination, the traditional association of snakes with bad luck in Sussex lies at the heart of its dragon legends. Like the dragons of Greek legend, the West Sussex dragon has inherited cultural associations with death and dark powers. While the Orient reveres the dragon as the great impartial power of the storm or as a beneficent rainmaker, West Sussex legend sent ambitious heroes after its dragons and baited them with outsize poisoned pies. If, as Jung asserted, dragon legends externalize the remnants of the older, ancestral reaches of the human unconscious, the killing or preserving of dragons in legend is a mirror to its native culture. When a medieval knight rode past Lyminster church and killed the Knucker Dragon of Lyminster Hole, he hacked in the name of structured faith and modern order.

Dragons are mythical spirits of earth and water and, standing at the summit of Bignor Hill in a December wind, West Sussex seems made of nothing else. Beneath the pure cold wind the plains are flooded with lake water, rainwater, river water. The winter sun breaks through the cloud bank and touches the swollen fields with a pale light. It has been a hard climb over grass littered white with tough rock, the wind shouldering us roughly every step of the way. The bare trees that line the steep track to the hill are snowy with blossoms of old man's beard. On Bignor Hill, with its winding sheep tracks, winter is in full fierce bloom.

The dragon of Bignor Hill sleeps now. His legend, scantly documented, is fading from the folk memory. All that remains of the scaled beast that terrorized locals and gulped sheep whole is a memory of a myth that once, long ago, the tracks in the hills were held in faith as the dragging coils of the monster's tail. We huddle down on the memorial Toby's Stone ('Here he lies where he Longed to be') and look out with watering eyes across the slopes of the dragon's hill to the raw earth of its Bronze Age burial mounds. This is hard, high, exposed ground, rough to the foot and bitter to the skin. The floodwater in the plain below and the white rock that bruised shin and ankle let us know that this is not a place to bring notions of an easy communion with nature. The dragon's hill is a wintry place of trial and burial: it holds itself taut against the modern eye and its quest for soft beauty.

I draw my coat around myself, remembering the Indian summer day at Cissbury Hill where the hunt began. There, ten miles across dry fields, hot beneath the yellow grass, a nest of legendary serpents guard a hoard of gold in subterranean tunnels. I sat in the grass in a cotton dress with my hands pressed flat to the earth of the hill, imagining the grumbling and stirring of mythical beasts. Heat poured from a cloudless sky, gusted upwards from the cooked earth. An adder crackled drily though the hedgerow at my back. A sense of displacement made my pulse seem to beat faster through my palms. I was a stranger to a new county, a new home, poised and pasted against the infinite promise and threat of an unfamiliar landscape. Pressing my hands harder into the earth, the blood's pulse became the reverberations of a heartbeat within the hillside. Here was something that knew my name.

Dragons are our dark halves. As symbols, they accommodate our fear of the dark, the unpredictable power of nature, our pagan ancestors. Protean, thrillingly other, dragon legends are a cultural fiction, a story that externalizes and organizes the disruptive and the murky. When the locals of Bignor made a dragon for the hill, they made it in awe and fear of the pagan burial mounds and great hill that stooped above their little village. The Bignor dragon was the spirit of the place – the wild high wind, the immensity of the hills above the village, the floodwater beyond the church door – given tooth and claw.

The dragon's breath blows wet and bitterly cold into our faces, and our blood responds with a warm defensive leap of circulation. Geoff fights to lay the map out straight on Toby's Stone, and I fetch nuggets of white flint and lay them at each

*A benevolent dragon, resting in
a West Sussex fireplace.*

corner. Struggling to trap paper under stone, I catch a gleam of
black in the chalky white surface. We turn the stones over in
our hands and find a hard, brilliant jet heart at the core of each
rock. I rub the black gleam with a numb gloved finger, thinking
of the winter blossom trees on the road to Bignor, the hard
climb against the wind on the way up the hill, of how the
bleakness of the landscape pares back the leaves and flowers of
summer, and makes us walk over stones and pull centrally
heated muscles in order to witness the communion of wind and
water at the hill's summit.

This, then, is the treasure that the dragon guards; a
blackberry-coloured jewel of silica in its shell of coarse rock.
Frozen in the wind on Bignor Hill, I find myself scrabbling
reflexively for metaphors to frame the motif of richness within
aridity, of the strength of confronting the wintry and the
exposed. I try to shout, but the wind batters in our ears and
Geoff can't hear me. I pocket the stone and let the words go.
Let them exist, like the dragon, always just beyond the sight of
the eye, and the compulsive grasp of meaning.

Myths and legends are perennial, but no dragon lives for ever. With the slow changes of a cooling sun, a legend passes its prime and grows, century by century, vaguer in the popular mind. At Bignor we found a legend in its last days, a slow death as inevitable as the passing from summer to winter. Five miles across the fields at Lyminster, a younger dragon breathes faintly in the deep water of the Knucker Pool.

The Lyminster Knucker dragon is said to have been killed centuries ago, but its legend remains integral to local lore. Strong Knucker beer is still brewed in the area, and packs a bigger punch than a swipe from a scaly tail. The villagers we spoke to knew that the Knucker's name is probably Anglo-Saxon, originating from the *nicors*, or water dragons, of *Beowulf*. This dragon's story, unlike the poor creature of Bignor, is well documented. The Knucker dragon lived in a pool close by the little Norman church and terrorized locals with its carnivorous raids on the local countryside, swimming as far up the river as Arundel to satisfy its taste for whole sheep and young damsels. One legend has the dragon baited and poisoned by an enormous pie, which was hauled to the Knucker Pool by a local on the back of a horse-drawn cart. The dragon died, but the hapless man swallowed poison from his hand as he drank a celebratory glass of beer, and died too. Another legend has the dragon picking off every young maiden in the countryside, until only the King of Sussex's daughter remained. The tombstone of the knight who killed the dragon and claimed half of Sussex and the princess's hand is said to lie within the church, his sword crossed on his chest.

We set off with high hopes to hunt the Lyminster Knucker on a grey December afternoon. The topography of this Sussex legend is satisfyingly compact, with village, church and dragon pool lying within a few hundred yards of each other. The legendary dragons of hills and woods have the power to enthral, but remain somehow impalpable, lacking the human scale necessary for a sense of immediacy. A legend that places a dragon in our midst juxtaposes the familiar with the foreign; beyond a turn in the lane, past the telephone kiosk, we may encounter the extraordinary something feared and longed for in the ordinary fabric of our lives. Buoyed up on legends, fortified by Sunday lunch, we rounded the narrow grassy path by Lyminster church, half hoping, with the parts of our brains that are always children, to see dragons.

A local couple had shown us an old aerial photograph of the Knucker Hole: a dark watery hollow, flanked by long, still trout ponds and a thick fringe of trees. With this picture in our minds, we rounded the muddy path from the village and found, where green water and hazel trees should have been, a seven-foot high metal fence topped by coils of barbed wire.

We circled the fence in silence, bitterly disappointed. Our tantalizing closeness to the site of legend and common lore, and the heavy fencing that all but barred our view, seemed a particularly nasty piece of irony. The ugly palings, reinforced steel and barbed wire that surround the Knucker Pool might once have been erected to keep something in; now, they keep local people and travel writers out. The Knucker legend, along with this, the rich site of folklore, is now owned privately. Beyond the fence, ducks and mallards called in the water, and the wind stirred drily in the withered hazels around the water. The place is desolate.

We stop on our silent circuit where the trees beyond the fence become sparser. I press my face hard up against the wire and see a cold pool of green water surrounded by withered reeds, wondering again at the ordinary sites for such extraordinary legends.

It is the depth of the Knucker Pool that distinguishes it as a site for legend. Tradition states that the pool is bottomless, and a local legend tells of village men tying ten bell-pulls from the church belfry together and dropping them into the pool without finding its bottom. In pre-Christian cultures a 'bottomless' pool was revered as a gateway to the underworld; the Knucker Pool, like many local wells and pools, may have been a site of ancient worship. In the medieval period, however, the bottomless mysteries of the Knucker Pool became conflated with the bottomless pit. The proximity of the pool to the church, moreover, made a fearsome dragon an excellent dissuader to would-be pagans.

Like the church bell-ropes, however, the Christian association of dragons with the devil cannot plumb the depths of the Knucker legend. Localized and colloquial as it is, the Knucker legend is drawn from an ancient international *mytheme* in which the king or tribe leader's daughter, the last fertile woman in the land, is saved from death in the water by the intervention of a fighting man. The myth has its source in the days when women were sacrificed to wells, streams and lakes in order to pacify the water spirits, who often took the shape of a dragon. The Knucker dragon is, it seems, a water spirit with mythical history as old as the telling of stories.

Beyond a private fence, legend is falling into sleep. We wipe mud from our shoes on dried sedge and listen dejectedly as a train labours through the fields, its vibrations dying tinnily in the barbed wire. There is something infinitely sad in this fence, and something, too, that is inevitable. We have come hunting stories of legends of a mythical beast, stories that were as impalpable four hundred years ago as they are to us today. There is more, to paraphrase MacNeice, than wire between ourselves and the dragon.

The fence obstructs us from occupying the site of the legend, but it is only a symbol of a more radical division between ourselves and our fictions. Somehow, oddly, this hideous fence saves us from the consequences of the quest for the story made real, the disappointment of reaching out for fairy food and touching only dry leaves. We climbed Bignor Hill and tramped through the mud to Lyminster Pool not to resurrect legends, but to witness their death. Dragons cannot outlive the common desire to give them life: with its telegraph poles and drive-in diners, West Sussex has no room for mythical beasts hobbling across its A-roads on clawed feet. We will tell new stories to frame what seems a perennial desire for ambiguity, but the dragon's day is done.

We take a last look at the pool as the afternoon light fades. The fence is high and strong, and may preserve the allure of the

Knucker dragon for a little longer. No researcher now can tell us that the 'bottomless pool' is a mere thirty feet deep, and that underground streams are the source of these dark green bubbles that suddenly disturb the water. We pause, watching the huge bubbles chase violently across the pool. In the dying light of the afternoon the green water seems to darken and thicken with ripples, as if a strong current of water or a large, dark shape were moving to the surface of the pool. In the moment before we turn away, the spirit of the dragon lives again. 'Tell stories,' it seems to say. 'Embrace the unknown.' We head for the car before the surface of the water breaks, preserving the precious lie.

'LET'S DO IT'

Nick Warburton

The last time I went to the Chichester Festival Theatre, the man who sat behind me started humming.

> Let's fall in love.
> Why shouldn't we fall in love?

At first there was something slightly disturbing about this. It wasn't that the humming itself was poor – it was, in fact, sweetly done and rather affecting – but that it was so inappropriate, so out of place. English audiences don't do that kind of thing. And few audiences are more English than those you find in Chichester.

The humming continued for a while and I became keen to see who was responsible. I did not, however, turn round to look. English audiences don't do that kind of thing either. On the whole, an English audience, and a Chichester audience in particular, doesn't kick up a fuss. It likes to sit unnoticed in the dark and avoid eye contact. And yet –

> Let's fall in love.
> Why shouldn't we fall in love?

To be honest, the level of disruption was fairly low. He had saved his humming until the first moments of the interval, just after the house lights had come up and while the applause was still fading. I suppose this was to be expected: it was unthinkable that a Chichester audience might subvert the play itself, except by the traditional passing of chocolates.

As I listened, I thought about my first visit to Chichester, as a student in the late sixties. We were near neighbours of the Festival Theatre and could take a short walk over Oaklands

Park to see John Clements, Alec Guinness and Peter Ustinov in Shakespeare, T.S. Eliot and Thornton Wilder. There were other links with the place, too.

During our first few weeks at college, we were thrown together in random groups and told to present a play. Our group met in someone's room and sat around for a while, looking at the floor and allowing the conversation to drift to other things. Few of us had much idea of what might work, and we wasted some time in indecision. Then Chris made a suggestion: 'I think we could do *The Royal Hunt of the Sun.* Does anyone know it?'

No one did, except by reputation. It was the great success of 1964, in the days when Chichester was host to the National Theatre. It told the epic story of Spain's conquest of Peru, and was rich in language and stunning effects; a bold, different play.

'All right,' we said. 'Why not?'

We were students. We had no idea why not. And Chris sounded very sure about it. He had seen more of the world than the rest of us, I seem to remember, and every surface in his room was covered with bits of a stripped-down car engine, which indicated purpose and enterprise. If he could put together an engine, I thought, he could probably put together a play.

'Well, then,' he said. 'Let's do it.'

He assured us that our production would be an historic one, both bold and unique. Having recently come off at the theatre over the road, it was virgin territory, untouched by the hands of amateurs. In fact, Chris told us, we would be giving its very first amateur production – a world première, of sorts. We were impressed. We weren't intimidated – we were students – but we were impressed.

We were not a large group. All the Peruvian warriors were played by girls, some of them very sweet and few of them blood-thirsty, and a West Country student called Mike represented the entire Spanish army.

Chris's directorial style was robust. I recall him running out of the gloom at the back of the hall to leap on stage and shout, 'It's no bloody good! It's no bloody good!' I recall, also, experiencing great difficulty with one line. It wasn't one of mine, but was spoken to me by a friend dressed as a monk. He played the part of Pedro de Candia, a Venetian captain, so I'm not sure why he was dressed as a monk. 'If de Soto raises his sword,' he had to say, 'he'll lose the arm that swings it.' We found this very funny. He couldn't say the line – and I couldn't hear it – without laughing. We didn't know why it was funny but it was, and it became impossible to say it. I have, some thirty years on, checked the line and discovered that I remember it perfectly. Which is odd: I usually have great difficulty remembering lines, even those I've written myself. (I once skipped a page and a half of a play I'd written, and watched with blank amazement as my fellow actor tried to make sense of what we were saying. 'He's rewriting my play,' I thought with some resentment as he fed me freshly minted lines which cleverly sketched in what I'd missed.) This line of de Candia's, however, stuck. In rehearsals, my friend rarely managed more than the first four words, but I have remembered the whole thing. I remember, too, Chris thundering towards us out of the dark. 'What's so funny? What's so bloody funny?' We couldn't make him see what was so funny. Cast changes were threatened, but there had already been cast changes and time was short. We had to find another way round the problem. In the end we coped with it by standing chest-to-chest, as directed, but turning our heads away from each other. I stared fixedly off stage-right while Pete, the monk, stared just as fixedly off stage-left. Sometimes it isn't only the audience who can't bear much eye contact. It was a strange confrontation – a non-confrontation, really – but I have a feeling that it worked. What was to us a device to avoid corpsing became to those who saw it a precise moment of rare tension. And the play was an unlikely success. People were moved, and we felt powerful. Or so I remembered it as I sat in the Festival Theatre listening to the man behind me hum:

> Let's fall in love.
> Why shouldn't we fall in love?

When the humming stopped, I risked a sideways glance and caught sight of a sensible brown shoe and a neat, corded, trouser leg. Clearly, the man belonged here.

Among theatre-going circles, Chichester audiences are famous – almost notorious – for their civilized bearing and conservatism. Their conversation is usually muted and polite. They dress up for the occasion and know what they like. They have a fondness for big-name stars of a certain substance, and for well-made plays which have survived at least fifty years. Up to a point, they are tolerant – they can forgive Shaw his argumentative socialism and make him a special favourite – but they are not likely to flock to Edward Bond or Howard Barker.

In their undemonstrative way these audiences have become quite influential. Anyone planning a season in the main house would be unwise to challenge their tastes too fiercely. This is not necessarily a bad thing. If one wants to be upset or disturbed in the theatre – which one does, sometimes – one can always take the train to London and visit the Cottesloe or the Pit. (These days, of course, one can also amble over to the Festival Theatre's slightly unruly younger sister, the Minerva.) But it is somehow comforting to think that there is still a home for these solid, tasteful old warhorses of plays in West Sussex.

Chichester Festival Theatre from Oaklands Park.

Not all audiences are as generous. Some hardened theatre-goers in London like to deliver running lectures on the meaning of the play to dimmer, quieter companions, and to anyone else within a five-seat radius. They like to hiss at latecomers and chastise whisperers. They'll sit unmoved through the blinding of Gloucester and yet be stirred to moral outrage if someone places an empty ice-cream carton under a seat. But something about Chichester subdues them. They flick mildly through their programmes and you'd hardly know they were there.

I realized this some years ago, when my train brought me late to a performance of Christopher Fry's *The Lady's Not for Burning*. I struggled into the theatre, sweating, breathing loudly and aware that I was fair game for the latecomer's hiss. It did not come. Neither was I subjected to lectures.

As things turned out, I could have done with a lecture at some point. The play I was watching confused me. The costumes were more or less right but the words weren't. It took a little while for me to realize that I was watching *The Taming of the Shrew* and that I was not, in fact, a latecomer, but an early-comer by a full week. But the good-natured audience was tolerant of such blunders, and I was able to wander the pleasant turf of Oaklands Park at the interval unmolested and as if I had every right to be there.

So perhaps that humming wasn't as inappropriate as it had at first seemed.

> Let's fall in love.
> Why shouldn't we fall in love?

Because I suppose I did. With the theatre. In Chichester.

FELPHAM

Vincent Hanley

No doubt about it – Blake walked here;
Crossed this beach,
Stood and watched the tide go out;
Between eye and word engraved
The shirred, pleated sea.
Inland, above green woods,
Angels descended in a bright column of light.
Labourers in fields shielded their eyes;
Villagers framed in doorways gawped.

Blake's Cottage, Felpham.

In Search of Boxgrove Man: Signs and Meanings in a Corner of West Sussex

John Saunders

My earliest impressions of Boxgrove were formed one summer's evening some years ago when the full might of the Chichester Evening League XI encountered the Boxgrove Cricket Team in a sixteen-over match. Chichester won the toss and batted. The local fast bowlers looked like blacksmiths and removed Chichester's frontline batsmen with crude efficiency. The fielding side seemed to be in tune with darker powers than those available to their more renowned visitors. As the match progressed and the dusk settled down, the cricket field became an echoing green. Children played in the trees on the boundary's edge. Their mothers, sensing the significance of the event they were watching, knitted. There was a general sense of fecundity and community. Cricket took its rightful place as a summer ritual. Before we left, we drank in the Boxgrove club bar, feeling as though we had been caught in a time warp. So it came as no surprise to me when news of Boxgrove Man began to filter through the national and local newspapers. I sensed that I already knew the site of the discovery – a mound adjacent to the cricket field.

'How long ago?' asked Maisie, my six-year-old daughter, in three words exposing the limits of my archaeological and anthropological knowledge.

'Thousands and thousands of years,' I answered.

'Is he older than Jesus?'

'Yes, much older.'

'Why?'

I've learned to ignore all questions starting with 'why'.

'How did he die?'

'Perhaps he died of old age'.

I was minding Maisie for the day and had planned an excursion to visit the site of Boxgrove Man. So, after breakfast, we set off on my bicycle, crossing Tangmere Airfield, past the Aviation Museum with its three planes and its toy tank, past the sign to the Bader Arms and on to the A27 roundabout where one sign says 'To Boxgrove and Priory/Halnaker' and another 'No Racing with Horse Drawn Vehicles'. Boxgrove on that autumnal morning was quite unlike the Boxgrove I had remembered. It is a neat, nondescript, one-street village with neat nondescript tiled-roof houses, bastioned with neat nondescript red-brick walls. Occasional lashings of whiter-than-white whitewash give testimony of a public consciousness and of public values. On the right there is a small grove of birch trees. There was, that morning, one pedestrian. She was walking a dog, I think an Irish terrier. I stopped and asked her the way to the archaeological site. She looked bemused and answered in an Irish lilt: 'I'm afraid I couldn't be too sure. They say it's not really in Boxgrove, it's more like in Halnaker. Yes, let me see. I think you turn right in Halnaker and go on up the hill. Then, I don't really know my left from my right, so you must listen carefully. Yes. I think you turn left at the road which leads to Halnaker windmill or is it right and then it's somewhere on the other side.'

'I know Halnaker windmill', said Maisie. 'I'll show you the way.' Then she added for the enlightenment of our informant, 'He's even older than Jesus.'

Halnaker is linked to Boxgrove by a half-mile tube of well-manicured greenery. And there, at the end of the tube, stands the village blacksmiths, incongruously out of place on a busy road with even busier roadworks. The blacksmith was out but we spent a moment surveying some of his handiwork – garden furniture and some garden statuary. One statue, green from its exposure to the elements, looks like Adam after the fall, weeping as he leaves paradise. Maisie didn't allow me to linger, eager now to show me Halnaker windmill. We rode on up the hill for half a mile, where a curt sign on the left-hand side of the road orders the visitor to abandon all forms of transport – cars, motor and other cycles. We crossed a stile and followed the path on until it reached the edge of a large, open field dominated by a view of the rigid white sails of the windmill. We squeezed through a fence and then trudged on to the top of the hill, the windmill growing taller and taller as we approached. Then we became aware of tinkling voices and discovered a party of very small children accompanied by a group of adults. It turned out to be the infant class of a local school, mothers and teachers shepherding some twenty tinies. I thought they were sure to know the whereabouts of Boxgrove Man, but they didn't. 'They are being very secretive about it,' the teacher in charge told me.

'A woman we met said she thought it was very near the windmill,' I said.

'It may well be, there are some quarries near here. You would be better off asking in Boxgrove. Try the post office.'

Halnaker windmill is a rural Taj Mahal. A plaque at the entrance announces simply:

THIS ANCIENT LANDMARK WAS RESTORED
IN THE YEAR 1934
BY SIR WILLIAM BIRD OF EARTHAM
IN MEMORY OF HIS WIFE

Strange that he, not she, is mentioned by name. Inside the windmill, names abound in an abundant testimony of more transient passion. The brick walls are dense with inscriptions: 'John loves Tracey'; 'Tracey loves William'; 'William bends over for Elton John'. The inner walls reach upwards for some forty feet. The more intrepid lovers have somehow written their inscriptions half-way to the top. But the brickwork is flaky and most of the signs are illegible. It was a lovely clear autumn day. The fallow fields and woodlands of Sussex stretched out below us. We could see the spire of Chichester Cathedral and, smaller but nearer, the spire of Oving's church. 'Do you think he lived in the windmill?' Maisie asked. He? Sir

William Bird? Elton John? No, Maisie's thoughts had returned to Boxgrove Man.

On our way back, we stopped for a moment at the blacksmith's shop in Halnaker. Until the present incumbent took over a few years ago, the forge had been passed down from father to son from the early eighteenth century. Now there is little demand for traditional blacksmithing. The current owner is an industrial blacksmith, who trained with the airforce in Essex. He specializes in designing and making wrought-iron furniture. Metal sculpture is something of a hobby. In the early days of the Boxgrove excavations he had met some of the archaeologists at the nearby pub, the Anglesey Arms. He told me that he had attended occasional celebratory barbecues on the site, but he seemed reluctant to reveal its location. I hinted, but didn't ask directly. Halnaker, he told me, means 'half naked'. I thought of Poor Tom. And, oh yes, he hadn't heard of Boxgrove's cricket team and was far too busy even to think of playing cricket.

We then cycled back to Boxgrove, stopping at the post office, which seemed to be the centre of community life. Here there were no Boxgrove men. There were, however, a number of Boxgrove women. Much of their conversation that morning might have been scripted by Jane Austen. Not for the first time, I felt that I was an intruder in the village. 'I'm looking for Boxgrove man,' I announced generally to the queue at the desk. Several of the women looked quite startled. 'I mean the site of the excavation,' I added hurriedly.

There was a longish silence. I received the distinct impression that the occupants feared that careless talk might cost bones. Then one of the women spoke: 'It's not actually in Boxgrove. It's up the road somewhere, nearer to Eartham.'

'So no one here's been there?' I asked. They looked ashamed and embarrassed.

'No, no,' said the spokesperson. 'You see, the site isn't open yet. It's being kept secret from the public.'

'Well we're going to find him,' said Maisie. 'Daddy promised.'

'Why not try the Priory?' one of the women suggested. 'It's just across the road and they have recently had an exhibition centred on the discovery. You'll find out all you want to know there.'

My first impression of Boxgrove Priory was of a ship, a great ship of faith, frozen on a sea of steel-grey waves. Then the waves, the gravestones of the dead who surround the priory on all sides, seemed to turn into tongues, their individual messages blurred but their collective message clear. As in Halnaker windmill, time has eroded most of the inscriptions. I found myself counting. Counting. Counting. How could a small Sussex village, now seemingly occupied by a few women and an Irish terrier, have so generously fuelled that graveyard. A small pamphlet on sale within the priory tells the story.

Now only a portion of the original priory remains. Domesday Book tells us that Boxgrove had the status of a parish and that there was a church there long before the Norman Conquest. When, early in the twelfth century, the priory was built as a satellite of the Abbey of Lessay in Normandy, all traces of this original church were obliterated. Through the next centuries, the priory grew and grew. By the year 1230 it housed nineteen monks. The architecture was altered to accommodate the expanding community, the Norman foundations giving way first to Transitional and then to Early English style. Building continued through the fourteenth and fifteenth centuries. Then came the Dissolution. Ownership passed into the hands of the Crown. Now, all that is left is the Church of St Mary and St Blaise, converted from what had originally been the quire, or monk's church. Though most of the surviving architecture dates back to well before the Dissolution, much of the more striking decoration within is modern: late Victorian and early twentieth-century stained glass; a reredos designed by Gilbert Scott; a statue of St Blaise; and a Virgin and Child by Professor Tristram of the Royal College of Art. In some ways the interior seemed to be almost too neat, too comfortable, too bourgeois – though the cold smell of stone hinted at an underlying austerity.

On the afternoon of our visit the priory housed two strikingly contrasting exhibitions. The one which caught Maisie's eye was by local schoolchildren. A large collage charted a journey from uncertainty to faith. It began with a child's version of the creation – a picture of sunny sky, green trees, a swing and a crowd of smiling faces. Underneath was the caption: 'JESUS GOOD OR BAD?' This was the start of a frieze which led on to a final panel where, above the caption, 'WANTED, FRIENDS FOR JESUS', new friends were commemorated in a display of children's faces made from paper plates.

The other exhibition recorded the discovery of Boxgrove Man. There were articles from daily papers and more learned journals, and a pictorial reconstruction which gave the impression that Boxgrove Men had spent most of their time practising the javelin. The most readily accessible write-up came in the *Independent*. Apparently, all that remains of Boxgrove Man is a tibia, or lower leg bone. It is the tibia of one who, in his day, must have been something of an athlete – a well-built six-footer accustomed to chasing and wrestling with his animal prey. He was also the heir to our first weaponry, the site abounding with signs of the making of flint tools. The article is accompanied by a small sketch of the archaeological site. It reminded me of those maps that occasionally attempt to give authenticity to children's fiction. In the sketch, time and space are condensed into a three-inch square. The detail provided hints at a grisly narrative. A number of the site's main discoveries are listed and pinpointed. The list includes a lion bone, butchered red deer remains, butchered giant deer remains, hyena bones, remnants of a butchered bear, remnants of a butchered rhino and a complete butchered horse. What is more, a cursory analysis of the tell-tale bone suggests that our Boxgrove Man might himself have been a victim of the flint butchers. As yet the cause of his death remains unknown, but there are both flint marks and animal teeth marks on the bone. Were Boxgrove Men and Women cannibals? Was he eaten by his neighbours, who then threw all his bones to the wolves?

Scanning by electronic microscope may – so suggested the *Independent* article – tell all.

'If they've only found a leg bone, how do they know it's a man and not a woman?' asked Maisie. We had abandoned cycling and were continuing our search by car.

'It's all a question of electronic scanning,' I explained. Following up other hints from Boxgrove villagers, we had explored the northern reaches of Tinwood Lane, ignoring the sign which says: 'No access for motor vehicles.' We had just driven down Thicket Lane, a lane that skirts the quarries at Eartham, and had stopped at the foot of the Downs at the incongruously named Mount Noddy. Mount Noddy is an RSPCA rescue centre. It is a temporary home for stray and homeless animals, mainly cats and dogs. The cats live in their own block called The Mews. The dogs occupy a number of less appropriately named huts. The centre finds homes for some seven hundred animals each year. It was their silver anniversary. Expressing a genuine interest in cat adoption, Maisie and I visited The Mews, where the more mature cats sat in individual cages mourning for their pasts, while the kittens, caged in litters, climbed up and down the netting, yelling for their futures. Mount Noddy costs in the region of £60,000 a year to administer and for a small sum it is possible to commemorate a departed loved one. A selection of small plaques on The Mews' wall pay tribute to a fidelity which transcends death. Most of the plaques seem to refer to pets, though one or two might be fondly remembering husbands. The Mount Noddy manager had heard of Boxgrove Man but knew nothing of his whereabouts.

'Try the quarry,' he suggested. 'It's only a stone's throw away.'

And at the Eartham quarry we were given two important leads. The first came from Arthur, an old cycling acquaintance who happened to be passing that way. I had met him at the time of the great Chichester floods when we had regularly shared information on the state of the rivers and the roads. Arthur knew the exact location of the site, information which he gave us in a hushed whisper: 'It's better to ask at the quarry and get permission first,' he said, 'then they won't get you for trespassing. It's private land, you see.' At the quarry we were given the name and telephone number of Mark Roberts, an archaeologist from University College London, who is one of the two directors of the Boxgrove Project.

On that autumnal evening, the excavation site seemed like a lost world. In the fading light the great mounds of gravel looked as though they had been carefully sculpted for a film set. It was easy to ignore the pylons, to take the distant rumble of traffic as the roaring of the sea and to imagine that the quarry had been the home of dinosaurs, not iron-jawed bulldozers. We clambered down the banks and made our way to the point of deepest excavation where there were unmistakable signs of distant, quite different worlds, as gravel gave way to sandstone, sandstone to chalk and chalk to sea sand. We were, I later learned, standing at the bottom of what had once been a massive cliff, now almost completely eroded away. And then the sun began to set. It had been a serene day, still and exquisite. But as the sun moved almost imperceptibly behind a western cloud, the whole horizon became a ring of red fire. Momentarily the surrounding terrain took on a quite unnatural glow, hectic emerald greens offset by lurid chocolate browns. And then, as the sun sank lower, both sky and landscape were drained of colour, leaving us caught in a sombre steel-grey light. A great gloom descended. I became aware that it was cold, very cold. Maisie, oblivious to the change, was totally absorbed by the slow deliberation of a tiny snail ascending a small blade of grass. 'Can I take it home? Can I take it home?'

That night I dreamed of Boxgrove Man and Boxgrove Woman, a crazy dream in which the gravestones in the Boxgrove Priory reappeared as milestones charting a journey through space and time, from then to now. Somehow Arthur, master of the floods, shared the roles of God and Noah, and Mount Noddy and its inhabitants were remnants from Mount Ararat. I woke having succumbed completely to the dream's

Seated figure on square steps: Henry Moore.

logic, convinced that I had solved the mysteries of creation by reconciling Genesis with Darwin.

In the days that followed, the dream faded and the divide widened. My search for Boxgrove Man became something of an obsession, an obsession fed by claims of the discovery of the 'missing link' and by the reassessment of the dating of the Big Bang. In my spare moments I skimmed through encyclopedias, learned articles and children's guides in an endeavour to place the discovery of the bone into some kind of meaningful context. Boxgrove Man (now fondly known as Roger) lived in West Sussex some 500,000 years ago. His tibia is thought to be the earliest discovered fragment of European Man. However, it is unlikely that he is our direct ancestor, though we may both be descended from a common antecedent who lived in Africa some 100,000 years earlier. Roger is probably an ancestor of Neanderthal Man, who evolved about 250,000 years later, surviving until extinguished by *Homo Sapiens*, on the move from Africa, round about 30,000 BC. All these timescales seem insignificant when we consider current theory on the datings of the missing link, dinosaurs and the Big Bang. With the aid of a pocket calculator I tried to scale down my newly acquired knowledge into a manageable form. If we condense the whole of time into a single year, imagining that the creation of the universe took place on 1 January, then, according to revised Big Bang theory, the first signs of life (algae and bacteria) took hold on the planet towards the end of July. The first dinosaurs appeared on 21 December, becoming extinct late on Boxing Day. The missing link came and went at about 7.00 p.m. on New Year's Eve. With about half an hour to go before midnight, Boxgrove Man roamed West Sussex and Christ was born when the year had no more than six seconds to go. And to think that before Darwinism took its hold, it was generally accepted that the universe was only six thousand years (or eighteen seconds) old.

'THANK YOU FOR TRAVELLING NETWORK SOUTH CENTRAL. WE APOLOGIZE FOR THE LATE ARRIVAL OF YOUR TRAIN.'

Brian Caws

If literature is defined as the ability to coin memorable phrases – and there have been worse definitions – then King George V's terse comment about Bognor, made during his last illness and employing effectively the techniques of assonance and alliteration, would earn him a place in any history of English literature. If, dear reader, you are not familiar with the phrase in question, there will be many who will enlighten you, particularly if they come from neighbouring Chichester.

The phrase springs most easily to mind in January or February if you happen to join the band of commuters on the 0642 train bound for London and scheduled to arrive at Victoria at 0819. It won't. Even if it started on time, there will be a cow on the line at Amberley or frozen points at Pulborough or leaves on the line at Littlehaven. The Sussex commuters are well aware of all this. They are patient and resigned and cold. West Sussex prides itself on being a beautiful rural county, and so it is; it is also a commuter county, and a substantial number of its inhabitants, far more than those who labour on the land, travel regularly to 'town' to earn their daily bread. This review of Sussex, therefore, follows one of the commuter routes: Bognor–Barnham–Ford–Arundel–Pulborough–Horsham–Crawley–Gatwick, and then out of West Sussex into the metropolitan heart of darkness. There is an alternative route, but that goes through East Sussex and the less said about that the better.

The journey begins on a cold winter's morning at Bognor Station. Bognor Station is not the worst in the world (have you ever changed trains at Crewe?) but, despite some vestiges of Victorian elegance, it is not the most beautiful building in West Sussex – only marginally more attractive than the Royal Pavilion in Brighton, East Sussex. It is also not one of the luckiest, having been destroyed by fire in 1899 and seriously damaged by lightning and fire in 1995. Its genteel melancholy, however, forms a suitable background to the journey into Cobbett's 'great wen of all'. Seasoned travellers always choose the side of the train away from the sun, on the days when there is a sun, and therefore, unlike P&O to India (POSH), the sensible way to travel on this line is POPH – Portside Out, Portside Home. The sun, of course, is not the main irritant. On later trains you need to be aware of children (three to five years) who move, predictably and with an inevitability worthy of Aristotelian dramatic theory, from awe to awfulness, via boredom, within fifteen minutes. Chattering adults come next.

All these are minor horrors with which many Sussex people are reasonably familiar, yet there are many compensations. The purpose of this little essay is not simply to catalogue grievances, for, in the true traditions of travel, the journey through West Sussex to London can be a pleasant, relaxing and occasionally even an uplifting experience. It is possible, of course, to separate yourself from it and a book is certainly useful if you are travelling after dark. Tastes vary but, for me, the best type of book is a collection of extracts or short essays. Alan Bennett's *Writing Home* is a good example of such a book; Alistair Cooke is another writer ideal for such occasions. On trains (or off trains for that matter) it is pleasant to spend time with writers who know what they want to say and say it. A wobbling train – and Network South Central trains do wobble, it is one of their hallmarks – is not the place to experience the kind of writing described sardonically by Stella Gibbons:

> I found, after spending ten years as a journalist, learning to say exactly what I meant in short sentences, that I must learn, if I was to achieve literature and favourable reviews, to write as though I were not quite sure what I meant but was jolly well

going to say something all the same in sentences as long as possible.

Unless it is dark, however, and you have to insulate yourself from screaming children and snoring adults, it is better simply to look out of the window. R.L. Stevenson expressed the point perfectly:

> Books are good enough in their own way but they are a mighty bloodless substitute for life. It seems a pity to sit like the Lady of Shalott, peering into a mirror, with your back turned on all the bustle and glamour of reality. And if a man reads very hard, as the old anecdote reminds us, he will have little time for thought.

It is always a mystery to me why more people do not look out of the window, particularly as the scene is always changing as the train passes through rural Sussex, through semi-industrial Sussex, through suburbia and finally into the centre of London. Let us take the journey the reverse way, out of London. The best time for this is twilight – the time of day that Saki described as 'the hour of the defeated'. There is a sense of romance and mystery about a great city at this hour, with the mixture of lights and shadows. As the train passes over the Thames, the illuminated bridges and the towering office blocks and flats achieve a beauty and a mystery of their own. It is almost the opposite of Wordsworth's view, early in the morning, but it is easy to feel the truth of his phrase about London's 'mighty heart'. In the gathering dusk, East Croydon, an ugly arrangement of commercial towers, becomes a fairyland of lights – stone castles inhabited by toiling gnomes. Railway stations, too, are interesting and ever-changing places with a story in every group and even more in the solitary figure standing a little apart from the rest. Think of the number of films set in a railway station; read the opening of Graham Greene's *England Made Me*.

Gatwick Airport has all the glamour, some would say all the tedium, of a major airport, and, like East Croydon, is perhaps most impressive at night. 'Change here for stations to all parts of the world', as a regular guard on the service regularly remarks to the irritation of all the other regulars.

It is as the train moves south, however, that the Sussex dweller begins to appreciate the special attractions of the county. Fresh air – really fresh air – begins at Horsham. The first view of the Downs, something to relish on every trip, is at Pulborough. Belloc's phrase – 'so noble and so bare' – describes them to perfection, while E.V. Lucas sums them up even more succinctly as 'the symbol of Sussex'. And so to Arundel, with its cardboard cut-out castle on the right, and, on the left, away on the hill, a far glimpse of the little village of Burpham. If you want literary associations then Arundel and Burpham will

Arundel Castle – from the London train.

certainly supply them. Mervyn Peake began his first novel, *Titus Groan*, from a three-roomed damp cottage on the bank of the Arun, Arundel Castle providing the visual inspiration for Gormenghast Castle. It is not difficult to make the connection from the window of the train, particularly when the castle is shrouded in mist. He returned to Burpham in 1943 to finish the first draft of *Titus Groan* and is buried in Burpham churchyard. On his gravestone is carved a line from one of his poems: 'To live at all is miracle enough.'

This is not Burpham's only claim to literary fame. The village, remote and ending in a cul-de-sac, is an ideal place for a literary retreat, and John Cowper Powys spent time there in Warre House, which he bought for £500 in 1902. He was not very popular with the villagers, who resented (and destroyed) his 'Trespassers will be prosecuted' notices, and he seems to have preferred America, but he did write most of his novel *After My Fashion* at Warre House. A lesser author but a more popular member of the village was Tickner Edwardes, a writer of romantic novels celebrating basic, even primitive, passions in rural settings. A good example of this type of thing was *The Honey Star*, a tale of stormy emotions on a Sussex bee farm, but the most well-known, partly because it was made into a successful film, set in Burpham in 1921, was *Tansy*. This was the story of a beautiful village maiden who becomes a shepherdess. It is certainly such books, along with Mary Webb's *Precious Bane*, set in Shropshire, that Stella Gibbons had in mind when she wrote her parody, *Cold Comfort Farm* ('Sussex, when all was said and done, was not quite like other counties'):

Adam Lambsbreath, alone in the kitchen, stood looking down unseeingly at the dirtied plates, which it was his task to wash, for the hired girl, Meriam, would not be here until after dinner, and when she came she would be all but useless. Her hour was near at hand, as all Howling knew. Was it not February, and the earth a-teem with newing life? A grin twisted Adam's writhen lips. He gathered up the plates one by one and carried them to the pump, which stood in a corner of the kitchen, above a stone sink. Her hour was nigh. And when April like an over-lustful lover leaped upon the lush flanks of the Downs there would be yet another child in the wretched hut down at Nettle Flitch Field, where Meriam housed the fruits of her shame.

Be this as it may, Tickner Edwardes was justly proud of book and film and, having taken Holy Orders late in life, finally returned to Burpham as its vicar, retired there, wrote a number of excellent books on country life and (and this is real immortality) founded the village cricket team. He died at Burpham in 1944, aged seventy-nine, and, like Mervyn Peake, is buried there.

Four miles north of Arundel is Bury and Bury House, the fifteen-bedroomed mansion of John Galsworthy. Galsworthy wrote several novels, including the last of the Forsyte series, at Bury and in one of them, *Swan Song*, describes the country around Pulborough very accurately:

> . . . flat meadows all along, that would be marsh in the winter, he would wager, with large, dark red cattle, and black and white and strawberry roan cattle; and over away to the south, high rising downs of a singularly cool green, as if they were white inside.

The train sensibly avoids Bury Hill, however, keeping to the plain and crossing the River Arun at Ford. To wait for the train at Ford Station on a winter's evening is an experience in itself, reminiscent of Will Hay's classic film *The Ghost Train*. On to Barnham, where the train usually divides ('Customers should make sure that they are in the correct portion of this train' – panic) and then the final few miles to Bognor ('Where this train terminates' – it being difficult for it to do anything else; 'expires' might be a better word). The beauty of the Arun Valley and the Weald has been left behind, even if Bognor has its own peculiar charm.

The train journey from London to Bognor and vice versa is, therefore, full of interest for anyone with eyes to see. The landscape, changing with the seasons, the varying forms of wildlife, including the human variety, and the movement through a county that is still supremely England. William Blake's 'green and pleasant land' is still an appropriate description here and H.V. Morton's view is still tenable: 'If ever a foreigner asks me to show him something which is typically English, I shall run him down to Arundel and walk him through the park.'

Surely it is better to look at it all than to bury oneself in, God save the mark, the *Daily Telegraph*?

HOLDING THE SEXTANT AND THE PEN: SAILING THE SOUTH SAXON SHORE

Francis Curtis

So through the Downs into the Channel again and back on my
way to the sea of Sussex, and to the shores which may be
drowned and swamped for a while by alien townsmen, but will
keep their own counsel and in due time will rise again.

(Hilaire Belloc, *The Cruise of the 'Nona'*)

It's always *towards* at sea rather than *to*. This form of travel is
a notoriously unpredictable and consequently dangerous affair.
Murdoch Mackenzie's 1786 sailing directions for navigating
the Looe Channel south of Selsey Bill are explicit:

To Sail through the Looe, and in the deepest Water over the
Cross Ledge, keep the top of that Hill in the Isle of Wight,
called Little See Mee just open to the Southward of Culver Cliff:
and take care not to shut, or open, any more of it, but
endeavour to keep about one half of it in sight. Observe, that in
coming from the Westward with Flood tide, and but little Wind
the Flood sets obliquely across the direction of the above Mark,
or towards Boulder Bank, which circumstance, must be
particularly attended to, when to the Westward of the Cross
Ledge, for without a commanding breeze of Wind to keep the
Mark on, there is great danger of being set upon the Boulder
Bank, by the direction of the Flood.

Mackenzie's list of unpredictable particularities – wind
strength, visibility, depth of water under the keel – could be
continued almost indefinitely when considering travelling at
sea. The Looe Channel is still unpredictable in 1994. Travelling
is also an experiment with time. Paul Theroux made this point
during his circumambulation of the British coast in *The*

Kingdom of the Sea. So today would see my continuation of a passage begun in Brighton Marina yesterday, nudging the South Saxon coastline towards Portus Adurni, or Portchester. Waves of travellers, voluntary and involuntary, have approached, skirted, landed and departed this coast over the centuries. I was in part an eighteenth-century traveller on this occasion despite the month of April and the year 1994. The passage was to some extent an opportunity to explore the accuracy and information contained in a number of charts which I had studied and which dated back to the 1780s. Photocopies of these, carefully rolled up in cardboard tubes stowed under the chart table, made fascinating comparison with current Admiralty charts. Were the former still valid? How could the twentieth-century mind interpret them? An east–west coastal passage closing the shoreline with reasonable wind strength, direction and good visibility was what I had hoped for and so far that is what I had experienced.

The rain had eased off, time to get moving. I was sitting in The Vectis tavern in West Cowes, always my first port of call on the island. Nothing much had changed since the last time: as soon as you stepped down from the High Street you saw those laminated strips at different heights on the walls, dated commemorations to battles against the tides. The Vectis was regularly flooded by the Solent on a strong, wind-assisted spring tide. The beer barrels upstairs and a surfboarder captured in black and white also proved it. Not much chance of flooding today, however, as a moderate southerly was veering west.

'I can't help you there, I come from Ryde.'

This statement came from the lips of a Vectian swallowing the last of the pint I had just bought him. Our conversation had been perfunctory and strained. He was waiting for the bus to Ryde. I had seen three arrive and depart since we had started talking. Only the excitement of an alleged handbag snatch minutes before seemed to interest him. Normal for Cowes, never happens in Ryde. He knew I was an 'overner': tourist, visitor, holiday-maker on his island, temporarily. Tomorrow I would be gone.

Yes. My visits to Cowes were frequent but temporary. Last night, as I coaxed *Calypso* past the Chain Ferry, the ebb was running at nearly three knots: I was fortunate to stem the tide. Keeping on track after rounding the Prince Consort buoy with a Red Funnel ferry blotting out my horizon hadn't been the brightest spot of the day, either. The travelling was through time and space: Victorian Cowes with Osborne House overlooking the Medina and the Prince Consort buoy marking navigable water. None of this had been visible to help Vespasian as he occupied the Isle of Wight or *Vectis* in AD 43–50. He needed to secure his southern flank before moving west to subdue the Britons in their hill forts at Dorchester and beyond. Classic Clausewitz. His galleys, effective only as long as muscle power held out, probably made it into the Medina rather than Bembridge but the foreshore contours are lost to us now. Today, Cowes is navigable at all states of the tide, Bembridge not. But nearly two thousand years ago? What was it like then? The unpredictability of maritime travel mirrors the diversities of historical circumstance.

It seemed a long time since yesterday morning when I'd taken on twenty gallons of diesel at Brighton Marina fuel pontoon at 0815. Steering 240 Magnetic I had set genoa and main at the Black Rock buoy with some difficulty. *Calypso* was pitching in a swell with hundreds of miles of fetch from the Atlantic. With Shoreham Power Station to starboard, Chanctonbury Ring at 235 metres was easily visible as I closed the coast with a moderating wind. Since it was also beginning to back north-westerly, giving me more weather helm, there was more optimism for the task to hand. Littlehampton Harbour soon appeared abeam, so I was able to fix my position with relative ease and begin figuring out the next series of manoeuvres. These were to take me back to the beginning of the nineteenth century in time as easily as I had now sailed the twenty-odd miles west from Brighton. Littlehampton passed under my starboard quarter and the outlines of Middleton-on-Sea and Felpham hardened into view.

Another time, another Sussex traveller, another coastline but

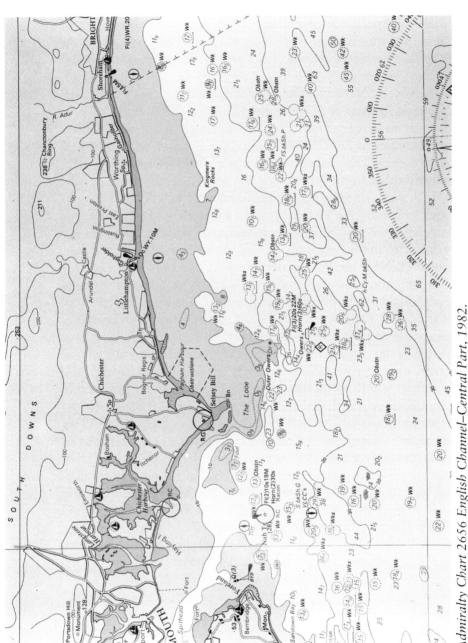

Admiralty Chart 2656 English Channel–Central Part, 1982.

somehow similar? Percy Bysshe Shelley's body in its smart sailor nankeen trousers with a copy of Keats in the back pocket was washed up on the Italian shore in the Gulf of Spezia in July 1822. I had always suspected that man's judgement. The drowning is generally presented as heroic bad luck, but I preferred to read it as the inevitable consequence of arrogance and ignorance at sea. Shelley, together with his two companions in *Don Juan*, a twin-masted vessel of twenty-four feet, foundered in a storm. The poet obviously had no idea how suddenly and ferociously the vicious Bora, ducting cold air catabatically from the Alpi Apuane into the Adriatic, could appear. Nor, presumably, how rapidly the Scirocco could emerge from the south. Shelley's jottings on wind directions relative to the boat's head, which I had examined years before, revealed little awareness of the complexities. *Don Juan* was carrying too much sail when it went down, held on against local advice and probably sailed with a dangerous ballast ratio. Ironic that Shelley, this 'infant in a boat without a helm', whose poetic imagery was drawn so massively from the weather, should be immune to its effects. There was a coastal connection between Spezia and Sussex, however. Shelley had extensive Sussex connections, from his birth and early childhood at Field Place near Horsham to his grandfather at Goring-on-Sea. The Admiralty Pilot above my chart table ushered in a further connection. I risked the stinging wasp of green foam to glance at it again:

> Dangers eastward of Bognor Regis–Buoys–Middleton Ledge is a low ledge of rocks extending from the coast about 1½ miles eastward of Bognor Regis Pier; the outer part of the ledge, which lies about 8 cables offshore, has depths of from 4 to 6 feet [1.2 m to 1.8 m] over it.
>
> Shelley [R]ocks, about half a mile southward of the outer extremity of Middleton Ledge, have depths of less than 6 feet [1.8 m] over them. There is a passage with a depth of 9 feet [2.7 m] between Shelley [R]ocks and Middleton Ledge, but no vessel drawing more than 6 feet [1.8 m] should navigate at low water inshore of Shelley [R]ocks and Winter Knoll.

Shelley Rocks? I'd seen them marked on the chart dozens of times, surely a valedictory by some sensitive Admiralty surveyor to the manner of the poet's death on a foreign shore. Shifting my eyes from the Admiralty Pilot on to the compass and then shorewards, I noted that Middleton church was bearing 330 Magnetic: I handed the genoa, bent on a small working jib which, when backed, kept *Calypso* hove-to on the rising tide, and set to work. A voice echoed in my ears as self-reflexively as Shelley: 'D–e–e–p one!'

Had I made a ghastly miscalculation with an *alastor* grinning over my shoulder? The sounding should be deeper. Stupid idea to use the lead on this mad-brained Shelleyan scheme. Just switch on the echo sounder and benefit from the technology. But that would ruin the point of all this. I concentrated again, making sure the safety-harness was snapped tight. The lead zipped forward, cutting the water as neatly as a fretsaw: 'M–a–r–k two!'

Safer! *Calypso* bore off on a prepared reciprocal while I coiled the leadline, but just as I was ready to solve this particular puzzle the VHF suddenly pinged into life, offloading unwanted decibels into the cockpit. The measured tone of Solent Coastguard could have been calling out bingo numbers: 'There is distress working on this frequency. No other calls are permitted. Please keep off.'

Another voice clipped in: 'We have no other vessels in the area so we've launched the lifeboat. Over.'

There was damn all I could do about it. Apart from scanning the horizon for parachute or red flares I did keep off, mindful that marine VHF is not a CB chatty piece of equipment for bumbling inconsequential gossip but life-saving gear. I concentrated and initiated dozens of mental calculations about *Calypso* to check my safety. Leeway? Tidal set? True wind direction and force? EP and distance run? How much under the keel? It wasn't an entirely relaxing situation with the wind increasing and an east-going tide. Middleton and Felpham gave way to the conspicuous Queensway flats in Bognor Regis, with the pier clearly visible and Bognor Rocks lurking below the water to the west.

Bognor Rocks. The football team is named after them and the Rock Hotel of Sir Richard Hotham's time once stood proudly opposite. This form of deterrent insularity was a curved ledge of fossil-filled calcareous sandstone extending seawards two miles to the east. If you stand on Bognor Pier at bright sunrise during mean low water springs, it is easy to believe you are witnessing the remains of a legendary town sunk beneath the sea whose bells toll intermittently during equinoctial gales. The rocks glow magenta and pink at nautical twilight, slab-set at awful angles. I became mindful, as *Calypso* drew steadily nearer, of what local historians had recorded about groundings here.

The Branch, captained by John Anderson of Sunderland bound for Southampton with a cargo of coal, had her mainsail carried away early in November 1862. She drifted down on the rocks, spilled coal onto the beach and was sold on the spot at auction. *The Canton*, laden with cement and shipping from London to Cherbourg, took in water on the edge of the rocks in the middle of August 1859 and foundered. The catalogue continues, although there is only one 'wreck' marked on the chart here. The square-rigged French schooner *Carnot* sprang a leak on Saturday 28 December 1912 and grounded on the rocks, pushed up the beach at Aldwick with cement and herrings in the hold. The archaeology of these, and other wrecks can still be detected at low tide west of Bognor Pier. Blocks of cement and rusting hoops from the *Carnot* reveal themselves at some states of the tide. A 'Pagham Phoenix', one of those D–Day concrete Mulberry Harbour components, floated off Pagham Harbour in May 1944, broke loose and was washed ashore on the beach at Marine Drive West. You can still see parts of it as you walk the beach. Hazardous to anything afloat, this twisted piece of faulty dentistry in the mouth of Aldwick Bay is marked on the chart. A glance at the chart following the VHF had set off this chain of associations amid calculations of a more disciplined kind. The wicked, black rocking-horse symbol – 'Wreck: showing any part of hull or superstructure at the level of Chart Datum' – leered at me sideways, daring *Calypso* to join the 'Pagham Phoenix'. Not today. *Calypso* was well off Bognor Rocks, heading to anchor under the lee of Selsey Bill as I speculated about the VHF distress warning. There was no means of knowing the type of distress that had come over the airwaves. Looking around it almost certainly wasn't caused by adverse weather conditions. A fire on board seemed a plausible explanation, I thought, making a mental note to check the storage life of my flares.

An hour later, *Calypso* lay contentedly to her chain off Selsey Bill within sight of the lifeboat station, well sheltered from the westerly wind. The station jutted its grey outline over the water, the familiar cocoon of a forty-seven foot Tyne Class slipway-launched lifeboat. While the station always reminded me of 1950s Triang model railway accessories, there was nothing dinky about its contents. I had been shown over this one last year. Two 425 hp diesels generating 2,300 rpm drove a self-righting vessel, with watertight bulkheads and bristling like a porcupine with electronic wizardry, 120 nautical miles without refuelling.

Thus comforted, I turned my attention back to the puzzle that the previous hour's casting of the lead was designed to solve. On examining the bottom sample on the tallow in the lead from this morning's encounter, I drew back my thumb sharply. The Shelley myth exploded in a glinting flash of silver shell and blood-stained thumb. Adjectival rather than substantive, the Shelley Rocks due south of Middleton church were simply rocks covered with shells, some of which were firmly impregnated, like myths in the unconscious, on the tallow. I rifled through the now jumbled assortment of cardboard tubes on the cabin floor for a dimly remembered reference. This was it: William Heather's 1797 Spithead chart marked, in delicate curving italics next to a circle of black dots representing the seabed, 'Shelly Rocks'. William Heather had published his survey in 1797 as the five-year-old Percy Bysshe played at Field Place, Horsham. . . . My romantic yearnings for the Spezia–Sussex link collapsed under the weight of Byronic realism.

Certainly a shifting spectrum of fact, myth and legend inhabits this coastline like the fishy opacity under *Calypso*. Selsey Bill and Pagham Harbour have more than their fair share, and this coastal journey was confirming it. I was anchored in the Park, now submerged land but formerly a medieval deer park carved out of the forest. It was here that St Wilfred established a monastery and taught the Saxons how to fish. William Camden asserts that the ruins of a thriving Saxon community, now identified with the Houndgate, Street, Barn and Park rocks, could be seen clearly under the water during the sixteenth century. Layered upon them, however, in some mad marine Mycenae were numerous obstructions, the most recent being the Second World War Pagham Phoenixes, wire-swept to known depths, which peppered the Park like buckshot.

Hauling my inflatable up the steep shingle beach under the lifeboat station was exhausting but worth the effort. The shingle overwhelmed the groynes. It sloped to the water at sixty degrees, ample proof that the Felpham Sea Defence Committee eight miles east was on to something with its demand to councillors that proper research into coastal erosion between Shoreham and Selsey Bill be carried out. The scouring effect of the tides, which alternately undercut and shifted sand and shingle, was plain to see. Littlehampton-registered trawlers bobbed up and down on their moorings like Louisiana oil donkeys, black cones rigged in readiness for tomorrow's catch. Bill House, with its tiled turret, rose above the skyline. I walked towards it across a flat wasteland adjoining Grafton Road.

Cutting inland along Seal Road – Selsey was formerly Seal's Isle – I crossed the main Hillfield Road that runs due south, along Clayton Road and West Street, until I reached the coastguard station. The station across the road rose, naval grey, into the sky. Its forward-raking windows betrayed no human presence.

Returning back across the site of Pontin's to the lifeboat station, a series of tithe maps, which I'd looked at in the West Sussex County Record Office, prompted further associations. I took in *Calypso* for a minute. She was held in stiff clay under thin gravel on a hefty thirty-pound CQR anchor. Under that was Gibbet Field, so named from the 1740s when the bodies of John Cobby and John Hammond, smugglers belonging to the notorious Hawkhurst Gang, were hung in chains. Hanged in Chichester at 2.00 p.m. on 9 January 1748 for the brutal murders of William Galley, customs house officer, and Daniel Chater, shoemaker, the bodies hung on a gibbet 'where they were seen at a great distance, both east and west'.

At that time the point of the Bill was considerably further south than it is now. I had on board a photocopy of Joseph Avery's 1790 chart, which shows an elevated cliff with extensive foreshore at latitude 50° 40″ 0′ N., the present latitude of Culver Cliff on the Isle of Wight. Even allowing for the shifting calculation of latitude over two hundred years, *Calypso*, in company with these trawlers and the lifeboat, took the water above eroded land where chained skeletons had creaked in the wind. A signal station, part of the early warning system against invasion attempts, had been sited on the tip of the Bill in Signal House Field, adjacent to Gibbet Field. The story of the Chater–Galley murders is commemorated for the traveller in Broyle Road, Chichester, by the Smuggler's Stone. This soft granite stone, unaccountably erected facing westward against prevailing winds guaranteed to efface its script, stands nearly opposite the newly built Sherburne House and along the wall of the former Military Police Headquarters. Five feet high, four across and twelve inches deep, the monument is 'a memorial to posterity, and a warning to this and succeeding generations'. The warning hasn't been heeded, of course. In 1994, cannabis instead of Cointreau, the *Poseidon* was boarded in Littlehampton harbour by HM Customs 'and a number of arrests made'.

Musing on the fate of Messrs Cobby and Hammond was a distraction from the proper business of keeping an eye on the inflatable, now buoyant on the incoming tide. It gyrated like a helicopter blade for some seconds before I achieved some slow, crabbed progress back to *Calypso*. That night passed in an agony of half-hearted anchor watch and smuggling dreams on the Selsey–Felpham coastline. The rhythmic thud and rasp of three-quarter inch calibrated chain woke me up and dulled my brain simultaneously. The wind tuned the mizzen halyards into a one-chord guitar. Sound and motion, the mariner's most important early warning systems in darkness and fog, kept me in half-awake limbo. Light began to seep around the curtained starboard quarter port, turning to grey until a chilly dawn eventually broke. With the kettle whistling its head off I tuned into the Solent local forecast for today's venture through the Looe Channel. Having held and swung minimally to anchor off the Bill, I aimed to follow Murdoch Mackenzie's eighteenth-century sailing directions.

The Looe tide race off Selsey Bill saves the mariner an extra fifteen nautical mile slog outside the Owers. The temptation is Janus-faced because there is no sea room to manoeuvre; the sea is invariably broken with sharp wave formations and foam-flecked overfalls produced by the Pullar and Boulder Banks lying off the Mixon rocks. The Admiralty Pilot warns that the Looe

> is only suitable for small vessels with local knowledge; no seaman should take this passage without plenty of daylight before him. The course through the western entrance across the Brake or Cross Ledge between the Street and Pullar buoys is about 097.

In other words, *Calypso* had to thread through a gap only two cables wide. Linford Christie would do that in eighteen seconds flat. The pilot assumed a west–east passage, but I was intending to sail east–west: the reciprocal course at 276. This looked too northerly to me. How did the Admiralty give directions in Nelson's time, and could I follow them? I looked back to Murdoch Mackenzie's 1786 sailing directions and considered them word by word, yet again:

> To Sail through the Looe, and in the deepest Water over the Cross Ledge, keep the top of that Hill in the Isle of Wight, called Little See Mee just open to the Southward of Culver Cliff:

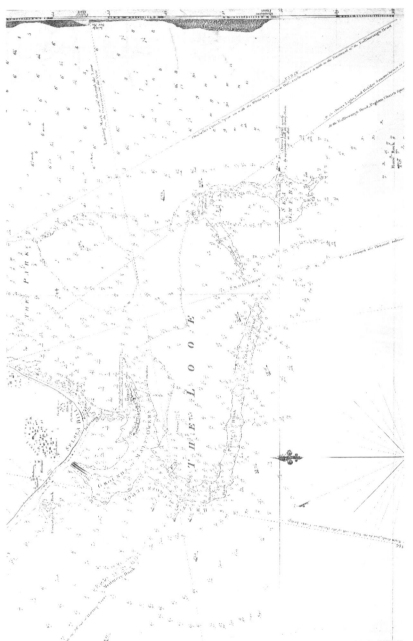

Survey by Lieutenant Murdoch Mackenzie of Owers, Chichester and Emsworth Harbours, 1786.

and take care not to shut, or open, any more of it, but endeavour to keep about one half of it in sight. Observe, that in coming from the Westward with Flood tide, and but little Wind the Flood sets obliquely across the direction of the above Mark, or towards Boulder Bank, which circumstance, must be particularly attended to, when to the Westward of the Cross Ledge, for without a commanding breeze of Wind to keep the Mark on, there is great danger of being set upon the Boulder Bank, by the direction of the Flood.

In 1786 a safe passage across the Brake Ledge depended on a clearing bearing of Culver Cliff and Little See Mee hill to avoid the danger of being set down on the Boulder Bank. Joseph Avery's 1790 survey repeated these directions but introduced the refinement of a position line through the Looe on an east–west passage with the instruction 'Cardinal's Cap & Culver Cliff in one', that is, in line, written on it. The bearing looked about 272. Would a course through the Looe with a large hill (Cardinal's Cap) rearing above Culver Cliff and a smaller one (Little See Mee) to the south still give safe passage? Were these hills visible, let alone recognizable?

A high bank of castellated, thickening altocumulus over the island warned of an Atlantic depression moving my way. *Calypso* unzipped the green astern on the west-going stream in a comfortable eight-knot wind which had veered easterly overnight to give near ideal conditions for the attempt. I gasped up and down like a manic squeezebox trying to pinpoint the Boulder buoy under the lee of the genoa. Soon it appeared with the red Street can buoy just glinting in line with the forestay about a mile away. Visibility was good but the island still thirteen miles distant. I certainly couldn't make out Culver Cliff. So much at sea is only apparent: apparent wind versus true wind, compass true versus compass magnetic, speed over the ground versus speed over the water. Messrs Mackenzie and Avery didn't have to control a blob of mercury on the bathroom floor called *Calypso* single-handed and follow sailing directions at the same time. They had a couple of seventeen-year-olds sixty feet up on the maintop with twenty-

twenty vision. Something showed up against the grey. The sea was as confused as I was. The echo-sounder, compensating somewhat for Mackenzie's extra help, flicked a black ribbon around the display to show an average of eighteen feet under the transducer. At a boat's speed of five knots I was suddenly whisked between the Street and the Boulder. The bow scissored the sea ahead to divulge, through the eyepiece of my monocular, a momentary sun-exposed image. This was a streak of feathery white framed in grey curves. It plunged out of sight, a salty epiphany as tantalizingly unrecoverable as Little Bo-Peep's sheep. That was the nearest I got to the eighteenth century. I discovered later that another contemporary set of directions and transits warns the mariner to take note of Little See Mee Not hill, not to confuse it with Little See Mee. Point taken. I saw not, making Victorian Cowes later that day against the ebb after a brief foray into Bembridge Harbour.

The Cowes–Ryde bus timetable didn't seem to worry anyone in The Vectis any more than the steady drizzle of that depression now arriving in Cowes. I crossed on the Chain Ferry back to the marina. Tomorrow's passage on to Portchester needed careful planning, with some tricky tidal calculations to consider. This cruise was almost over. You can glide along the coast of Sussex and Hampshire by car or powerful motor cruiser with a few gallons of diesel, but crabbing this coastline under sail is a salutary experience. It reveals a stubbornly resilient culture in the region. Salt and sea are embedded on the coast. The official history of the Sussex County Cricket Club is entitled *From the Sea End*; The Rocks have constant faithful support every Saturday. From Vespasian onwards, whoever has approached or departed this coast has had to deal with the likes of the Felpham Sea Defence Committee or the Standing Conference for Problems Associated with the Coastline: drilled throughout history to distinguish the apparent from the real, to monitor and evaluate the shifting myriad of impressions the inhabitants of the South Saxon coast are obliged sometimes to see and sometimes to see not.

Three Poems

Hugh Dunkerley

Natural History
(Kingley Vale Nature Centre)

These are the casualties,
the ones who never made it
to the tangled safety of the other verge,

their lives seeping away in ditches,
or who, racked with toxins,
lay under bushes, uncomprehending,

as a million suns
burned through their bodies.
Now they're pinned and labelled,

a gruesome catalogue of flattened rats,
voles and squirrels
frozen in contorted agonies.

The roe faun like a mummified foetus,
its too-long legs
twisted at impossible angles.

An emaciated husk, a label tells me,
was once a green woodpecker
that must have died of starvation,

its balding plumage almost colourless.
A pinboard is lined with skulls,
pebble-sized finches and sparrows,

the curlew's beak like a huge needle,
four times as long as its head.
And below it, something I can't make out,

a thin tube of dried-up flesh
ending in two big-fingered paws
and a ruff of fur.

A faded card is lying beside it.
'Mole', I can still read, 'found July 1969'.
I lift the tube onto my hand.

It weighs almost nothing.
The long claws are like fishbones.
Whatever ate it, turned its skin inside out

like a glove, stripping away everything
except this stubborn spine
and these feet with their wrinkled, human palms.

Deer
(Selhurst Park, South Downs)

In the semi-darkness
two deer materialize on the path,
shadows loosening themselves
from the surrounding trees.
I freeze as one, ducking its head,
begins to graze,
while the other, tremblingly alert,
tunes its swivelling ears
to the rustle of my coat,
the loud ticking of falling leaves.

My breath plumes the air
and the deer moves its head
seeking confirmation
of something it senses,
a faint edge of the human mingling
with the mould-wet smell of leaves.
I inch forward, the mud
sucking noisily at my shoes;
half a mile away a car is murmuring
its way up a hill.
Then a dog barks
somewhere beyond the deer
and both are suddenly flickering away
in a gliding bound.
For a moment they come to rest,
keyed-up, electrified;
then melt soundlessly into the trees,
their white rumps bobbing into darkness.

Another Summer
(Tangmere Airfield, June 1994)

Sussex stifles in the heat,
fields raked by sun,
the panting trees
weighed down with their greenery.

Your uncle points to hangars
that have evaporated like mirages,
runways overrun by battalions of wheat.
He remembers pubs he drank at,

wobbling back through the blackout
on Air Force issue bicycles
– 'it's a miracle no one was killed' –
and flogging Canadian cigarettes

and military blankets smuggled out
under bulky greatcoats.
In the dark of the museum he recognizes
a few grainy photographs,

young men leaning nonchalantly on Spitfires,
cigarettes dangling from their lips,
two washing their feet outside a tent,
and fighting over the soap.

He can name the ones who died,
slipping from radio contact
somewhere over Normandy,
or who, their planes already burning,

crashed short of the runway,
the fuel erupting in a balloon of flame.
At the gift counter he toys
with a shrapnel paperweight,

telling the woman he was stationed here
and how nothing but the skylines seem the same.
Outside the light is blinding,
the car like a furnace.

We drive away towards Chichester,
its spire still a marker,
although everywhere the trees have grown,
that summer trapped in their rings.

WAITING

Hugo Donnelly

I came to Fittleworth towards the end of the sixties, as a teenager. My mother had died the previous winter, and I was in the absurd position where, as a minor, I was not permitted by law to remain living in my own house. After considering the various options for my resettlement in Northern Ireland, I decided on flight. A well-meaning friend secured me a post as a waiter at the Swan Hotel in Fittleworth through an agency in London, which had had the job on its books for some time and was glad of a taker. This form of work would secure me food, money and a roof over my head until I came of age to inherit the money from the sale of the house. I left school, added two years to my age, packed a suitcase and took off.

One afternoon of summer heat I stepped off the 1405 from London Victoria onto Pulborough Station, perched on a hill which overlooked a row of shops, and then a flat river meadow stretching far back to a ridge of smoky grey hills. I had visited England only through novels, and I remembered that it was here, in an isolated farm on the marshy sweep between Pulborough and the South Downs, that *The Day of the Triffids* reached its climax. Somehow it was a comforting thought. A taxi on the sloping forecourt took me the two miles from Pulborough to Fittleworth, a village cast in green shadow, where high trees closed in as the car curved down a road between raised walks of neat English cottages. Then there was the Swan Hotel, diving into view on a curve of the road, its windows empty in the afternoon silence. I paid the cab and walked through the dark entrance door to the hotel. This was to be my home for almost a year.

Fittleworth is reputed to stand on the oldest road in England, and the Swan Hotel is the alleged site of the original settlement. Here, a Saxon wanderer named Fitela (mentioned in *Beowulf* as the dragon-slaying son of Sigemund) threw down his bundle one day, checked out the river and the ford, the fertile watermeadows and the rising, sheltering woods to the north and south, and set up his *weorth*, or enclosure. By the fourteenth century, Fitela's *weorth* had developed into two stone cottages, later amalgamated into a single building which served as an inn for coastal travellers and the herdsmen who drove the milking-herds to and from the meadows. From 1536 it was a coaching inn, and provided a change of horses for the royal couriers of the King's Post en route from London to the coast, before the long climb up the South Downs at Bury Hill. The main hotel building stands at right angles to the road, facing north, and imposes itself suddenly and dramatically on the coast-bound traveller. Turn a bend in the long street of Lower Fittleworth, and there, unexpectedly, with its red-tiled façade and moss-covered roof, complete and ready, is the Swan Hotel. The road doesn't so much seem to pass it as to flow into its forecourt and settle there, like a river basin. E.V. Lucas,

The Swan Hotel, Fittleworth.

Lamb's biographer, thought it the most ingeniously placed inn in the world. 'It seems to be at the end of all things. The miles of road that one has travelled apparently have been leading nowhere but the Swan.' Until the road was widened in the thirties, a wrought-iron gantry straddled the road with the inn sign – a huge pillowy swan – fixed to the centre of the boom, visible in both directions long before the inn itself. For the road-weary traveller, it was impossible to resist or ignore.

Entering the Swan was like wandering into a tavern in a Wessex novel, a place of low beams and sloping floors, oak panelling and creaking joists. There was a small restaurant (ten tables), a lounge festooned with my employer's collection of corkscrews and policemen's truncheons, and a spartan public bar where beer cost less. Back in the sixties there was still a fairly rigid class division in drinking arrangements. Locals from the council houses up at the Fleet made the snuff-brown bar their own. The lounge bar was used by the clutches of coastal travellers who had come slightly off the main route to explore Petworth, stopping off for a drink or a meal in the Swan (the main coast road, the A29, is now two miles east of Fittleworth). Then the other Sussex types: landowners with beefsteak cheeks and expensive shoes; retired military men who resembled Snudge from *The Army Game* and drank gin and bitters with the manager (ex-RAF) at his niche near the counter flap; merry andrews in white flannels who tipped out laughter easily and stood back from the counter, in a line, arms folded, legs at ease, like the slips in a game of cricket. In Goodwood week the serious gamblers rolled in, with serious drink habits that kept the Swan awake till the early hours. But the clientele the Swan traditionally valued were artists. The typography of Fittleworth, with high hills to the north and south, areas of thick woodland, a river meadow, various clays supporting various outcrops, leans heavily towards the picturesque. Fittleworth is traditionally known as the Art Village and the Swan is the artist's pub, renowned for its sensitivity to the imperfect money-sense of Bohemians. The coffee lounge is known as the Painted Room, where hard-up artists left what critics hope is not their best work on the wooden panels around the walls, in lieu of payment for bed and board. Constable stayed here and painted Fittleworth Mill, and each good day of the year a crop of resident artists dragged their chairs and easels from the Swan to the footpath by the public road to paint the millhouse after Constable. The mill was by then in private hands, and no longer functional, a tall, handsome building with brown weatherboarding in the shelter of even taller cypresses. There was a twin mill-race, and at times a spate of water came foaming into the lasher and swelled the green millpond, where strands of willow hung mournfully over their own reflections. Or the artists walked up to Hesworth Common, a high sandy heath with tall pines thin as pencils swaying in the breeze, and through the pines a view of the whole range of the South Downs from Chanctonbury Ridge to Cocking laid out in a line. They joined fishermen along the banks of the Rother, or walked on to sketch the seven-arched medieval bridge that carries the road over the Rother at Stopham. They painted the barns and the meadows and the High Street and the Swan, or painted each other painting, easel to easel, until poor light drove them into the Painted Room for sundowners.

There was no one my own age in the village. Two boys slightly younger than me lived down the way, across the river by Fittleworth Mill. They dressed like illustrations of boys in wholesome English classics, and looked as if they might get up to the same high jinks as Jennings and Derbyshire. The river lay before us like a frontier, and I never saw them on my side of the water. But I did have two regular companions during my stay in Fittleworth. One was a terrier mongrel, a skinny, wiry old thing with rusty tearmarks on his cheeks and a permanently dejected manner, who adopted me as a friend. Each day when lunch was over and I came through the darkened bar into the protestant hush of the afternoon, Old Mournful would be sitting there on the forecourt, his pink tongue beating in the heat, waiting, and when I walked past he would slowly rise and wander after me, like a guardian with a melancholy duty to perform. He never once approached me, but always kept his distance about ten feet behind, like a Hindu wife. If I stopped, Old Mournful stopped too, and if I looked at him too long he started to get shy, and lifted his snout up to sniff the air, as if that was the reason he'd tagged along with me, rather than for the company. Whom he belonged to I never found out. We would part each day as we met. Old Mournful would accompany me to the front door of the Swan, and then sit on the forecourt, at his discreet distance, until I walked inside.

The other companion of this period was a temporary resident in the village, a tall man with a soft Scottish burr to his voice, whose name I cannot remember. He was an explorer, he said, resting between exploits, and his dark moustache and restless brown eyes reinforced the image of a nomad. I first met him on the narrow road through the woods to Coldwaltham, at the south end of Fittleworth. I was pondering the enigma of two dead snakes nailed to a tree by the roadside when I heard his step approach. As St Patrick had driven all our native snakes away, I was intrigued to come across two large specimens stapled to an English oak tree. Then I heard his voice behind me. 'Adders. This area is infested with them. That's a warning for light-shod ramblers to watch their step.' He leant reflectively on a gate and pointed his pipe: 'I've seen a heap as big as a bushel skip on a bank yonder, when they collect in the spring. More making their way to the heap. In the old days they were farmed for fat, taken from the adder's head and rendered down into antiseptic oil.'

True to the spirit of its founder, the dragon-slayer Fitela, the village had a rich tradition of snake lore. As late as 1860 there are sincere accounts of an 'audaciously large' dragon which would rush out of its lair in Fittleworth woods 'with a terrible hissing', to terrorize passing cottage people. The explorer lent me a book called *Some West Sussex Superstitions Lingering in 1868*, collected by Charlotte Latham from the cottage people of Fittleworth while she lived at the Old Rectory of St Mary's Church. In those days the village was still almost entirely insular. It was the rule rather than the exception, the explorer told me, that villagers never spent a single night away from their own home throughout their lives. Perhaps this ignorance of the big world might account for the puzzling slant of some of the superstitions (for example: *you must not collect hailstones. If they are put into a wineglass they always run through it, and leave a slop underneath*), and were interspersed with cures that showed a triumph of hope over reason (*for ague, eat seven sage leaves seven mornings running*). It was through the explorer, who had a passion for Elgar's music and had read through his letters and journals, that I learned about the composer's stay in Fittleworth. (I was under the impression at this time that Elgar was Scandinavian. But the name, like Fitela's, is pure Saxon, meaning 'Fairy spear'.)

Fittleworth is broken up into three separate clusters, and the most northerly part of the village lies across the

Brinkwells, where Elgar stayed from 1917 to 1921.

Pulborough to Petworth road at Halleluja Corner, where the church of St Mary's stands on a high mound. This is the old coast road to Wisborough Green. On the flat stretch of treeless road stands Fittleworth House, a gloomy mansion of grey stone down a long, gated drive, evocative of Manderley in *Rebecca*. Then the road narrows, and cuts into the soil of the hill so deeply that the roots of the trees break through the high, crumbling banks at head height, almost closing out the light. This is Fittleworth Wood. The first day I walked up there, with the explorer and Old Mournful, not a single car passed to break the silence. Chaffinches rattled in the leaves. Then three pheasants appeared from the undergrowth and kicked a path noisily through the verges ahead of us, jutting their necks back to keep an eye on us, wary of Old Mournful. I had never seen pheasants before, and was fascinated by their ancient, exotic colourings, a richer brew of the duns and reds of autumn debris strewn around us. We left the road there and walked through the spongy floor of the woods, Old Mournful trotting behind us, a sense of closed air in the amber-coloured gloom. Near the summit of the long, steep hill we came back onto the road and turned right, down a rutted sloping track. At the bottom of the lane, on the left, was Brinkwells, a large thatched cottage of grey stone which Elgar rented for several years. He moved to Brinkwells in the autumn of 1917, depressed by the war, depressed by his lack of creativity, uncertain about his future, and remained there, off and on, until 1921. Perched high above the world in Fittleworth Woods he could hear the flat boom of artillery fire from the battlefields across the Channel. But for Elgar (and perhaps for the explorer), Fittleworth was a place for repairing broken nerves.* He loved the woods, where mists hung in the dawn

---

* Kipling, another artist whose jingoism concealed a haunted, unsettled heart, also recaptured his demon amid the 'thickish mutter' of the Sussex Downs. Like Elgar, Kipling stayed at the Swan and left a note in the visitors' book in 1901, written either in triumph or frustration: 'Motored from R/Dean [Rottingdean] 30 miles in 3 hours.'

and nightingales sang at night, and felt an overwhelming sense of mystery in these surroundings. He wanted to stay here and become a hermit. Listening to the boom of that civilized carnage on the Western Front, where generals sacrificed battalions for boundaries of mud, Elgar regressed from the nightmare of history into the primitive timelessness of wood life. Parts of the village gave him what he called a creepy feeling of primeval things, and he roamed the miles of woodland for days at a time, studying woodcraft from the woodmen there, who cut chestnut for fencing and hurdles, larch for panels. He made footstools and doorstops, pen-holders and trays, and learned to make hoops for barrels. During the harvest he went out to the fields with his swop-hook and helped to glean the oats and clover with the local farmers. He made his studio in the garden, which looked down across the sloping wood, where the Rother glinted like mercury in the Arun plain, and the blue mass of the Downs rose above low hills against the sky. From here he could see the blot of Chanctonbury Ring, the most haunted place in England, where it was reputed that a sad ghost roamed in the afternoon with its head bent down, a white beard drooping, searching for lost treasure. Elgar waited for inspiration to come, and it did. At Brinkwells he composed music that was different from anything he'd written before. When she heard the slow movement of the violin sonata, his wife, Alice, traced its influence to the 'wood magic' or *genii loci* of Fittleworth Woods. At Brinkwells he also composed his cello concerto, and a violin quintet inspired by a cluster of gaunt trees on a plateau at the summit of the hilly fields above Brinkwells. There was a legend that a settlement of Spanish monks who lived here degenerated into pagan ritualists. One night, during some unspeakable impiety, a stroke of divine outrage turned them into trees, whose twisted forms and spectral movements found their way into the phonic weft of Elgar's 'ghostly' quintet. The legend of the impious monks was reputedly embellished by the writer Algernon Blackwood, who came to visit Elgar at Brinkwells, and whose supernatural tales I was familiar with at the time. Elgar had written the libretto for a stage version of Blackwood's prophetically titled novel, *A Prisoner in Fairyland* (1913), and was excited by Blackwood's belief in the possibility of a paranormal extension of consciousness. What might have happened to Elgar in these haunts of ancient peace is conjectural, for when he applied to buy Brinkwells from its owner his offer was rejected, and he had to make other plans. As Michael Kennedy says in *Portrait of Elgar* (p. 245) he returned there in August 1921, after the death of his wife, and found the same sense of mystical continuity, but the loss of human company left him feeling dead: 'I have tried to take up the old life, but it will not do so there's an end. I feel like these woods – all aglow – a spark wd. start a flame – but no human spark comes.'

*   *   *

Each night except Tuesday I take my stand in the restaurant to trade our excellent fare. I sweep up to greet the first customers of the evening, my black dickie crisp as an orchid below my scented chin, my cummerbund the pivot of a formal bow. For two? Certainly sir, certainly madam, flicking crumbs from a table with a chequered napkin (hoover later).

'He's the best young waiter we've ever had in that restaurant,' *says the manager, and this pumps me full of pride. I seat my customers carefully, reassuringly. I slide the chrome ring from their napkins and whip the air once, twice, with crisp white linen which I sink into their laps. Tucked up in my silk-seam pants and duck-tailed jacket, poised to listen, I write, I take orders. I smile now at this table, now at that, as I swing through the service-door (oil for that creak, sometime) three, four, five steaming plates balanced on my forearms. This customer, that, makes a sign. I come instantly, return a moment later with the bill discreetly folded on a saucer (no service charge: gratuities discretionary). I make a good impression on my customers. They are amused by my commitment* (still so young, yet so professional!). *They like my style. I perform my duties well, perhaps excellently. My forest wisdom has them on their knees with gratitude. Someone raises a forefinger, his troubled face rucked*: 'I need good fortune, old son. On my beam ends.'

'That the queen of night dart not malignant rays upon you, on the first day of her reappearance, you must immediately turn head-over-heels.' *He looks even more troubled.* 'Should you cut your nails on Monday morning without thinking of a fox's tail, then you will have a present made to you.' *His smile returns.*

Another wipes his foaming mouth with a napkin: 'Anything up your sleeve for hydrophobia?'

'A slice of liver of the dog that bit you, to be boiled and eaten. Incidentally, beg six sixpences from six young bachelors, make a silver ring for your wedding-ring finger. Cure for fits.'

Lady Jayne Jewell peers feebly over the menu at me: 'So gled to see yo. Can't see a bally thing. What's thet faw?'

'Poor vision. Apply the water that is found in the cup of the teasel. Alternatively,' *I open my other hand*, 'a spider live, rolled in butter, eaten.'

She eats the butter and turns with clear sight to the manager: 'Oh Harry, I'm so heppy. You've found a Merlin. Yo' didn't tell me, did yo'?'

'Bally gout!' *roars Brigadier Hardy-Roberts, Keeper of the Keys of the Queen's Household.*

'Nine mice roasted to a cinder, sir, powdered, sir, swallowed fasting in a glass of ale, sir.'

'Jolly D, Huge Joe. Set me traps right after the port. Really quite something, that chap! Thought all the chaps like that went west at the Somme!'

And the morning coffee in a china pot for Sir and Madam in the office, newspapers folded in my teeth:'Looks like a storm brewing up out there, Huge Joe.'

'Avoid the ash, it courts the flash. Beware the oak, it draws the stroke.'

He sets a mouth and jabs the stem of his pipe at my chest: 'Y'know, think I'll take your advice, Huge Joe.'

'Oh, simply the best ever,' *his partner rejoins, and I walk lightly for hours, the best ever, then crouch in my room (so hot, the paintwork on the sill smells scorched) behind the frowsy glass, cars baking on the packed forecourt of the Swan, Fittleworth, in 1969.*

* * *

I kept a diary at the time. It is the dullest record of any human activity I have ever read, repeating day after day the numbing ritual of waiting. For a seventeen-year-old who enjoyed company and had experienced moderate success as a rock musician, serving toast and Gentleman's Relish to Sussex brigadiers was not a life choice that would have occurred in the normal run of destiny. On my days off I went up to London, to the colourful displays of youth in the streets and parks. There was an endless party going on, and I moved among this harlequin tribe like an outsider, a spy, trim as a Mormon, tailored to wait. The world was wilder and more serious than when I'd last had the chance to look at it. In a couple of years, rock groups had metamorphosed from genial music-hall troubadours to committed thinkers, with major themes and concerns in their orbit, forging *concepts* from ganga and bagism and eastern meditation. My rural backwater began to feel unreal, a fake. The old framed photographs on the walls of the bar showed Fittleworth as a bustling, living village with a nest of trades, where children played with hoops in the road and the blacksmith, cobbler and weaver posed resolutely outside their places of business for the camera, determined to live forever. Drained of its industry by the towns, Fittleworth was now a decorative hamlet that thrived on silence, where The Old Forge and Weaver's Cottage were names on ceramic badges, private homes with geraniums in the windows and fat, slumbering cats on the sill. The railway station was derelict, closed during the Beeching cuts. The branch-line west to Petworth and Petersfield was torn up, and the track through the cutting in Tripp Hill was choked with brambles. No malt in the storehouses, no horses in the stables, where the stalls had rotted from the feet upwards and rusting bridles jingled on the bricks. It was sometimes the loneliest place on earth. At night, when the restaurant closed, I would walk up the winding street, the smell of the river in the air, and watch the colours that closed lives threw on the curtains. From the top of Tripp Hill I could see the amber glow of the southern coastal towns beyond the Downs, where the party was going on too. Or in the long, slow afternoons I would follow the Rother to Stopham Bridge across the water meadow, Old Mournful in tow. Leaning on one of the recessed parapets above the river, I would imagine that the blunt cutwater was the prow of a speeding ship, carrying me away against the tide from West Sussex. I felt lethargic and drained, my energies checked, like the snail that Linley Sambourne, then editor of *Punch*, drew in the visitors' book in 1892, with a poem:

> If seeing this and reason fail
> And Wonder says 'why draw a snail?'
> The wherefore is, as snails are slow
> So the Swan's guests are loathe to go.

Then a human spark did come, and fires, as the tribal jigs began in earnest across the Irish Sea. I came from a Republican border town in a valley in the Mournes, with a volatile political temper that had resulted in its reduction to smoking rubble on more than one occasion. It was a place that had thrived around the first canal in the British Isles, and went into decline when the railways came in the nineteenth century. In the late sixties it had the highest unemployment rate in western Europe. Now it had followed me across the sea in newspaper pictures and on TV screens. I was suddenly looking down those old streets again, night after night. Boys I knew from school were dancing like savages on car roofs while terrified drivers fled. Buildings were on fire. Smoky mobs gathered behind barricades and hurled petrol-bombs at B-Specials. I was suddenly the focus of a different kind of attention. I was sounded for my political opinions. Some applauded my prescience, a refugee *avant la lettre*. During the day, cameras panned shoppers on the High Street. There was Bridget Havern, and Maria Patterson who worked in the Florentine Café. Nora Bagnall from Derrybeg, her black hair tangled like a fey barbarian, was leering blithely into a million English homes. It seemed like an outrage, a joke at my expense. I was hiding somewhere in the world, and they had found me.

One day, the explorer went off to Tierra del Fuego. A week later, when I put my suitcase into the boot of a waiting taxi to take me to Pulborough Station, bound for London and home, Old Mournful, who had risen to join me from his accustomed spot on the forecourt, watched with a perplexed gaze as the car drove up the street and around the bend. Old Mournful vanished, the Swan vanished and, in spite of everything, I said goodbye to Fittleworth with a lump in my throat.

THE WILD(E) DAFFODILS

Ted Walker

On 8 March 1967, William Plomer wrote to me:

> How kind of you to remember the daffodils. Of course I would
> greatly like to see them if it can be arranged. And if it *can* be
> arranged I might – if you think it a good idea – ask the
> Colemans at Steep Down if they are likely to be at home, and if
> so, whether we might look in on them. . . . I don't really know
> them very well but they have always been very nice to me. They
> are a childless couple with a farm and, as I told you, they
> looked after Bosie Douglas in his last days. I should describe
> them as non-literary & none the worse for that.

The daffodils were wild ones. I knew of a remote track,
somewhere to the north-west of Steyning, beside which the
delicate flowers grew in golden, Wordsworthian hosts among
chestnut coppices. Paul Coltman, a good poet and my old
English master at Steyning Grammar School, had shown them
to me the year before, swearing me to secrecy. Only we and
the gypsies knew where they were, Paul had said. I wrote back
to William, eagerly agreeing to a meeting with the Colemans,
and suggesting that perhaps he might like to make the
acquaintance of my former teacher – about whom, for
William's amusement, I composed a sparky vignette. (At
school, Paul had been given to smoking herbal – indeed,
coltsfoot – pipe tobacco, often leaving a not unpleasant
fragrance of autumn bonfires in his wake.)
William replied on 20 March 1967:

> If . . . we can fit in the walk you suggest, that is a splendid idea,
> & we'll try & see Colemans, Coltmans, coltsfoot and fly
> orchids. I rather think the Colemans have some orchids on their
> land, but haven't ever been there in orchid time. (Last year I

wrote a short poem about finding & not picking orchids, described by me as rare, though they weren't all that rare.)

Surprised by an old guilt (as I rake over these events which took place nearly thirty years ago) I daresay I must own up to (at best) self-delusion and (at worst) overweening deviousness, for I now persuaded myself that if I effected an introduction between the two poets – both good friends of mine – then surely the guardian of secret knowledge about the whereabouts of Sussex wild daffodils would grant me at least his tacit approval to pass on this knowledge to a self-proclaimed non-picker of admittedly not very rare orchids. (As a sixteen-year-old schoolboy at Steyning, I had dug up the bones of a Bronze Age man – and his buckle – up on the Round Hill. First, I'd had to take up turf containing dozens of bee-orchids, which I'd been careful to replace afterwards. This was not long before, with the invention of the tractor roll-bar, they could plough up there on those precipitous slopes and grow some of the best barley in England. Also, years before the busybodies put a stop to such independently pragmatic and creative curiosity.)

As things turned out, I didn't have to betray a trust: William (for reasons I've forgotten) never did see those wild daffodils – though I did take him to see the Warnford snowdrops two or three Februaries later. Nor did he meet Paul Coltman. And I wasn't to meet the Colemans yet awhile. However, the non-literary, childless couple at Steep Down were still being alluded to tangentially in letters. They impinged. By the end of April (the daffodils now over), William wrote:

> Rupert Hart-Davis turned up & . . . I showed him an excellent new life of Wilde in French by Phillipe Jullian, who has just sent it to me. In the Introduction he alludes to me as 'grand spécialiste de cette époque' (that is, the nineties), but that is *tout mon oeil*. Hart-Davis tells me that Bosie Douglas's last words (at the Colemans') were: 'What won the two-thirty?' I don't think he ever backed a winner in his life.

Spring and summer passed, and it wasn't until 23 October that
the Colemans were mentioned again: 'I must try & go & see the
Colemans at Sompting in November. Would you like to go too, if
it can be arranged? We could perhaps meet at Worthing station.'
On the 26th, it was confirmed:

> I sounded out Coleman about our visiting them. He will
> welcome us, or rather, he and his wife Sheila will welcome us,
> either to lunch or dinner. I think lunch would probably suit you,
> as me, best . . . on Sunday 12 November. If you come by train
> [to Worthing] we'll get a taxi up to Steep Down; if you come by
> road, I'll cadge a lift from you . . . [Coleman] says they are
> going to 'an opening meet' on 4 Nov., and friends are arriving
> from Paris to hunt with them during the following week.

There's something that needs mentioning at this point in the
light of what follows. The evidence, contained in these and
other letters, is that by this time I was beginning to gain
confidence in my abilities as a writer. I was thirty-three, father
of four children. I had published two collections of poetry, won
two major awards and was earning large fees for my *New
Yorker* short stories. On the proceeds I had bought the house in
which I still live, a car for myself and a car for my parents. I
intended soon to give up my teaching job in order to go
freelance. ('I won't say, "Are you wise to make such a
decision?"' William had written, 'because, as I think you know,
I have great confidence in your gifts . . .'.) I was enjoying the
literary life and was proud to know literary lions such as
William Plomer. (He had befriended me, having urged the
publication of my work to the house of Jonathan Cape.) Also, I
often had in mind that, as an undergraduate at St John's
College, Cambridge, I'd dined in hall time out of number
beneath the Pickersgill portrait of my fellow alumnus
Wordsworth, for whom the wild daffodils at Ullswater had
meant (though I wasn't to know of this *aperçu* until much later)
what deprivation would later mean to Philip Larkin. I'd have
been embarrassed to admit this then, but I was tickled to death

by this frail literary coincidence. With (I trust) appropriate humility I was daring to believe that I might become at any rate a minor figure – a footnote – in the great tradition.

But I was also aware that ragged-trousered working-class lads like myself were still exotic *arrivistes* on the English literary scene in the 1960s. Good old William was endlessly encouraging: but his world was not quite my world. When I told him I was a part-time football commentator, he assumed I pronounced upon rugby; and when (because he loved to link his disparate friends one way or another) he told me that, like me, the Queen Mother (to whom he had sent my books) loved fishing, as I did, it was beyond his ken that casting for wild Scottish salmon was not quite the same as long-trotting, with worm or maggot, for roach-beam hybrids.

And so I was uncertain how I'd survive a social encounter with the huntin' Colemans after their week in pursuit of the fox in company with *le beau monde*. Not long before, I'd partaken of luncheon in the Café Royal with William and the Marchioness of Cholmondeley, whose poetry prize I'd won jointly with Stevie Smith. The Café Royal, I'd rightly assumed, was no greasy spoon or caff. However, where Oscar Wilde, Lord Alfred Douglas, Whistler, Frank Harris and their cronies had once foregathered had proved to be not so much a glistering and glamorous watering-hole redolent of *la belle époque* as an enormous congeries of dining-rooms booked months in advance by commercial travellers and such. (In Keats's *Hyperion* there is an allusion to a fallen Titan called 'most enormous Caf', which is how, ever since, I have always thought of that Byzantine, many-chambered eating-place. Arriving amid a crush of Rotarians, Flat-Earthists, neo-Keynesians and sundry other interest groups all seeking their appointed burrows, I'd inadvertently all but jostled Princess Margaret headlong to her specially spread red carpet. And an hour later I'd somehow sent my *baba au rhum* flying, fork-propelled and at great speed, like a soggy token from a surreal game of tiddly-winks, beneath an adjacent table in the red-plush and plate-glass mirror Grill Room.)

Duly, I picked William up at Worthing Central Station. He was, as usual, jokey, playful and anxious to put me at my ease. When I applied the handbrake outside the front door of the Colemans' house, we glimpsed the Colemans' hunters, their superb heads protruding above the half-doors of their stables. (I hadn't the heart to tell William how often I'd trespassed on the Colemans' land as a boy; how I knew their ancient rabbit warren on the top of their wooded hill behind Sompting as intimately as they.)

I recognized Teddy and Sheila Coleman at once. They had been a locally famous (and, to use today's word, glitzy) couple in the years immediately after the end of the Second World War. I would have been about eleven years old. The roads were empty and petrol was scarce, but the Colemans used to bowl grandly past our house at the scruffy end of South Lancing in what I think (I don't know much about cars) was a sporty and supremely elegant Jaguar SS, with hubcap spinners in the shape of that fascist image – a comma and an inverted comma combined. Luncheon was served (on gold plate) by a butler in a bum-freezer white jacket. I acquitted myself tolerably well. William's description of the Colemans as 'non-literary' had evidently been a kindly euphemism for rather dull – but, they were 'none the worse for that', given their kindly hospitality, I thought.

Coffee was served in a different room. A photograph album was produced, and I was shown a snapshot of an oldish gentleman posing between two gateposts. A hedge of euonymus stretched away in both directions.

'Do you know who that is?' Teddy Coleman asked me.

'No,' I said, 'but I do know those hedges.' In the lateish forties I'd trimmed them for 5s. during the Boy Scouts' Bob-a-Job Week. 'The Esplanade in Worthing', I said, 'but God knows who that man is.'

There was a pause, while the album was taken from my hands. 'That man is Lord Alfred Douglas,' said Teddy, 'and that house is where Oscar Wilde wrote *The Importance of being Ernest*.'

A few days later I took my camera to the Esplanade. What I found was a pile of hardcore. The house in which one of the masterpieces of English literature had been written had just been bulldozed to make room for a Gulf filling station.

Five years elapsed. During these years I acquired and avidly read the *Collected Letters of Oscar Wilde* (edited by Rupert Hart-Davis) and discovered how – precisely at the time when Wilde's reputation was at its peak – the egregious Marquis of Queensbury, Lord Alfred Douglas's father, was gathering evidence which would ultimately result in the great playwright's disgrace and imprisonment. Wilde had sought to evade the company of Bosie Douglas, first in Brighton and then in that villa on the Esplanade in Worthing, in order to have what these days is called 'space' enough in which to write his play. But Douglas had tracked him down. One morning they hired a boat and rowed to Littlehampton, picking up boys on the way. I imagined how, after coffee and a third or fourth fragrant cigarette, they'd passed through those gateposts flanked with the hedges I was to cut for a dollar a couple of years after Bosie died, his 2.30 bet down the pan.

Five years, I say. Then, in 1972, Worthing proposed a literary festival. This seemed like little less than effrontery, given that one could search in vain for much in the way of visible municipal recognition of Worthing's literary associations. Very well: there was an area of streets named after writers – who had nothing to do with Worthing; there was a plaque on the Richard Jefferies cottage in Goring; the Worthingian John Selden had a road named after him. However, the lovely little theatre in Ann Street had been razed in favour of a multi-storey car park; there was nothing to show that Shelley had published his first pamphlet here, or that Harold Pinter had written *The Caretaker*, also in Warwick Street (only a ten minute walk from where Wilde had written *The Importance of Being Ernest*.) A number of us Sussex-based poets were asked to write short poems (to be illustrated, in small poster form) about Worthing's literary figures. William's (about Hudson) characterized the town as 'unconscious' and

Oscar Wilde and Lord Alfred Douglas, 1894.

mine (about Wilde) as 'lacklustre'. On 14 December 1972,
William wrote, enclosing his poem.

> Well, here's a copy of my contribution. We're going to be very
> popular in Worthing for calling it 'lacklustre' and 'unconscious',
> & will I hope provoke a peevish complaint. That we *shan't* do is
> prod them into any lasting, public indication of their fortuitous
> association with O.F. O'F.W.W.

('Sails Oscar Fingall O'Flahertie Wills Wilde' had been the last
line of my poster sonnet.)

We had not yet done with Worthing. In March 1973,
William, Leslie Norris and I were the readers in a celebration
of the life and work of Andrew Young in an ugly church in the
town. There were few attenders. William wrote, on the 27th:

> I did wish a few more ears had been in the church. . . . Although
> poor Leslie was *piano* & I believe feeling very wretched
> the character of Andrew Young & his work came out very
> clearly. . . . Perhaps to speak of poetry in Worthing is rather like
> raising a banner marked Excelsior in a waste land. . . . On my
> way back to the hotel that evening a man asked me to direct
> him to Longfellow Road. 'It's a Longfellow that has no turning,'
> I said gravely.

Six months later, William was dead. To this day I mourn
him. Throughout Sussex there are places where I took him (or
had intended to take him) and places he alluded to, or wrote
about. I feel his presence whenever I drive a mere mile or two
from my front door. And (in no small part owing to his
influence and teaching) I feel the presence, too, of writers from
the past who have travelled my way before me: Keats, Larkin,
Collins and others in Chichester, near where I live; and,
elsewhere in the county, far too many to mention here.
Travelling is a matter of history as well as geography. While I
waited for William's train on Worthing Central Station, I
remembered how Parson Kilvert (whose *Diaries* William had
edited) had once waited here too. That pleased me.

I remembered, too, how, when I was confirmed by an Australian bishop in Hove parish church, I experienced little in the way of spiritual revelation. What had impressed me, though, was the notion of the laying-on of hands, generation through generation, in a direct line down from Saint Peter. Poets, I began to realize, can lay claim to a similar lineage. I knew Andrew Young in his old age; and Andrew had known all those Georgians, who knew Swinburne, who knew . . . who knew. . . . And thus, in not many moves, I could get back almost as far as Chaucer.

I was to consume another luncheon with the Colemans. I accepted Teddy's invitation, correctly guessing that I was going to be asked a favour. Would I bring such influence as I had to bear to get Lord Alfred Douglas's poems back into print? I left, after coffee, with an LP record of Bosie's address delivered to the Royal Society of Literature on 'The Principles of Poetry' in September 1943. At home, I reread the well-turned but lifeless sonnets, and I listened to his pompous lecture. Even if I'd had any influence – which I certainly hadn't – I wasn't inclined to urge republication of his stuff. It wasn't much good: he'd been a mischief-making, vindictive, litigious and spongeing creature all his life, and he'd have snubbed the likes of me. Why should I lift a finger on his behalf? And so I said no to Teddy Coleman.

But here's a curious thing. During that second visit to the Colemans, I learned that in 1945 (the year of Bosie Douglas's death) they had been living not at Steep Down but in the former presbytery in South Lancing. So I had been wrong, imagining Bosie living out his last days in that handsome farmhouse, writing his daily betting slips there. These days the Lancing Women's Institute has use of the presbytery on a Friday morning for their sales. I've taken my aged mother there on occasion to buy produce of this or that kind. While waiting for her to make her purchases (and, perhaps, buying a bunch of rhubarb for myself) I've had the strongest sense of Bosie's snob-ridden presence stalking about disdainfully among the homemade jams, cakes, pickles, plants and such. I daresay that in the spring there are daffodils for sale. They won't be wild ones. Wild daffodils (or Wilde daffodils, as I think of them) are exquisite, miraculous, fugitive, perfectly made true originals. Garden daffodils, by contrast, are loud, intrusive, obviously derivative, overblown and, if you ask me, somewhat '*bosie*'.

STRANGE AT BOGNOR

Patrick Garland

It was strange at Bognor. . . . Strange the sea was, so strong.

Oyster-smacks gaily bounce over Bognor Rocks,
FAN(N)Ys with pride cling to their squaddies' arms,
As brass-band music bangs and whistles up the Front,
Tweenies croon doubled over babies' prams.

Our boys in blues and reds, strong sea as white as pearl,
Nursemaids stirred to passion for their wounds,
A one-legged soldier roused by loving glances of his girl,
Long waves, small boats, blue sky, pier, sea-side sounds:

'The Moon shines Bright on Charlie Chaplin' –
But not on vacant arm or folded trouser flapping free;
A fox-haired man watches high tide advance
And soldiers tramping from an opalescent sea.

They can hear sea-gulls, walk the pier and music-hall,
But do not see his legions of the awful icy dead –
White ghosts from Festubert and Neuve-Chapelle
Flop from the surf and march on shore with murderous tread.

It is the whiteness of the ghost legions that is so awful.
(D.H.L.)

In March 1915, at the time of the battle for Neuve-Chapelle,
D.H. Lawrence left Shed Hall (a small cottage generously lent
by Viola Meynell) at Greatham, near Pulborough, for an
excursion to Bognor Regis by motor car. Later, he wrote about
it to Lady Ottoline Morrell. It appeared to have been a fine

March day, with fishing boats out at sea and invalid soldiers in hospital blues casually strolling with their nurses. 'I was on the pier', he said. But Lawrence could see only ghostly legions of soldiers from the Western Front tramping home out of the icy foam. Exactly at that time of year in France, the retreat had bogged down into a war of attrition between Festubert and Givenchy, and savage hand-to-hand fighting waist deep in mud at Neuve-Chapelle. In the same month, in the Gallipoli Peninsula on the Aegean Sea, a task force of British troops and men of the Australian and New Zealand Army Corps were preparing to land at Anzio Cove.

'GOODBYE TO THAT BELOVED BOGNOR': VIRGINIA WOOLF ON THE SOUTH COAST

Jack Kissell

In February 1897, the fifteen-year-old Virginia Stephen (later to become the novelist Virginia Woolf) spent five unwilling, unhappy days at Bognor with her sister Vanessa, her half-sister Stella Duckworth and Stella's fiancé Jack Hills. The reason for the visit was to enable Jack to recuperate from a minor operation and to allow the engaged couple an opportunity to further their relationship. The visit was dogged by bad weather. After arrival on Monday 8 February, a series of dismal excursions took place in a muddy, rain-swept landscape. The party cut short their stay, returning thankfully to London on Saturday 13 February. The prospect of this return was noted in Virginia's journal: 'Thank goodness! Another week of drizzle in that misty, muddy flat utterly stupid Bognor (the name suits it) would have driven me to the end of the pier and into the dirty yellow sea beneath.'

It is tempting to take these dismissive remarks at face value and to regard those five unhappy days as having no significance in her life. Such comments might seem obvious to a modern reader familiar with Bognor's less than flattering image. In 1897, however, the resort was a refined and genteel place with a 'season' extending throughout the year. The comments of Rob Shields on Victorian Brighton apply equally to Bognor and to the Stephen party that arrived in February 1897:

> There was a genuine love of feeling that one was standing safely in the teeth of a gale. . . . The daunting force of Nature and a sense of the puniness of human endeavour produced an exhilarating experience.

Thus, postcards of Bognor in the 1890s frequently show dramatic images of large waves breaking over the sea wall, threatening to engulf seafront hotels.

If, however, we look beyond those dismissive comments ('utterly stupid Bognor') and examine more closely her five unhappy days on the coast, we will discover significant patterns of experience in the development of Virginia as a woman and a writer. To make those discoveries we must first consider the sources of the anger and frustration that characterize her response to the visit. Second, we must examine the three distinct methods by which Virginia tried to make sense of her writing holiday: a written journal, photography and an extensive programme of reading.

Why was Virginia so irritated by her stay at a respectable resort? First, the excursion disrupted the enjoyable round of visits, plays and lectures that constituted her family life in London during a period when she was recovering from the trauma of her mother's death in May 1895. Second, she was called on to perform the thankless task of chaperone to her half-sister, resuming a role she had earlier played as a young child. Third, at the time of the Bognor visit Stella had assumed the role of substitute mother to the Stephen family while at the same time offering to Virginia, as she was to write later, her

> first vision . . . of love between man and woman. It was to me like a ruby; the love that I detected that winter of their engagement, glowing, red, clear, intense.

This embodiment of a love 'so lyrical, so musical' was offered by a woman who was at the same time 'too remote for real companionship'. Furthermore, in complete contrast to the studious, voracious reader Virginia, Stella Duckworth 'seldom read a book' and had a 'gentle impassivity about books and learning' (Schulkind, 1985). These, then, were some of the familial tensions that led to Virginia's anger at visiting Bognor, an anger which permeates the journal entries leading up to the visit and which virtually dominates the diary entry of 1 February.

Having seen some of the potential causes of the friction and tension which permeated the Bognor visit, it is revealing to consider in turn the three methods – writing, photography and reading – which Virginia used to make sense of her experiences by the sea. First, then, her written journal records factual details of arrival, places visited, meals and shopping excursions. In error she notes the address of the lodging house as '4 Cottesmore Crescent' instead of the correct 4 Cotswold Crescent, a mistake clearly showing that her mind was still on London and Cottesmore Gardens, a street very close to her Hyde Park Gate home.

In addition to recording daily routine, a journal also highlights events of special note. In Virginia's Bognor diary she singles out for special attention a dismal excursion by horse and carriage to Arundel Castle; hilarious attempts by her sister to load a camera under a pile of bedclothes; and a mud-spattered bicycle trip with Vanessa across wet roads and muddy fields which met with the derision of local schoolboys out for a walk. This last incident is a significant and early example of Virginia's hypersensitivity about her appearance and her tendency to attract amused attention in open public places. Such events, and the resulting phobias, played a key role in her development as a woman and as a writer of prose fiction, as Roger Poole so cogently demonstrated in his psychological study, *The Unknown Virginia Woolf* (1978).

The language of this early journal, in sharp contrast to the highly literary diaries of 1898 and later, is flat and prosaic. Slight heightenings of style can be noted only when Virginia refers to three physical objects from which she derived comfort and security: an armchair given her as a birthday present by Stella on 25 January ('How I wish at this moment that I could find myself in my comfortable arm chair in the nursery at home!'); Lockhart's *The Life of Sir Walter Scott* (1837–8), a birthday present from her father ('10 beautiful little blue and brown gilt leathered backs, big print and altogether luxurious'); and the Frend box camera which was delivered to Bognor on Friday 12 February ('in a new box, all rubbed up and beautiful, smelling strongly of Jargonel!'). These three treasured objects were closely connected with the processes of interpreting and making sense of life. Thus, a camera records impressions of the moment; reading is a means of mediating the experiences of others; and the armchair represented for Virginia a secure location for reading and writing. Lacking her own room, she had at least a chair of her own.

Perhaps of greater significance in her written record of experience at Bognor is Virginia's unconscious comment on the dynamics of the group. Throughout the visit she notes different permutations of the visitors. For example, 'Nessa and Stella went to the station', or 'Cycled with Nessa once up and down the esplanade'. However, the most persistent grouping is that of Vanessa and Virginia separated from Jack and Stella. This sense of exclusion is noted on no fewer than six occasions, typical entries being 'Stella and Jack made a pretense [sic] of walking on with us but soon turned and went back alone' and 'Jack and Stella sat in the dining room together and Nessa and I in the drawing'. It might be argued that such a grouping and sense of exclusion would be obvious when a Victorian engaged couple was chaperoned by younger siblings, but the point being made here is the strong emphasis placed on it by the journal writer, an emphasis later to be increased by photographic record.

If we now turn to the photographs that Virginia took on her Bognor visit, we will find confirmation of the patterns of experience established in the journal. Virginia was a keen photographer. She was closely involved in the photographic process which led to the two images taken on Bognor beach (see illustrations). In a letter to her brother, Thoby Stephen, on 1 February she acknowledged receipt of his gift of 'two beautiful packets of superfine celluloid films'. On 12 February her journal noted the loading of the camera and taking two photographs on the beach 'but the light was bad and I do not know whether they will come out'. On 14 February she noted: 'After tea Nessa and I developed in the night nursery. One very good one of Jack and Stella on the sands, the others all dim

Jack Hills and Stella Duckworth on Bognor beach, photographed by Virginia Stephens, February 1897.

and under-exposed. The batch of films is 1515 m.' Clearly, then, Virginia was actively involved and knowledgeable about the photographic process. She acknowledges her ownership of the images produced.

In analysing the two photographs taken on Bognor beach, we could usefully bear in mind the comments of Val Williams on snapshot photography:

> It would perhaps be useful to realign snapshot photography and to establish it as a documentary rather than an explicitly casual form . . . its preoccupation with the family and with the passage of time would allow its role as a marker and a recorder to be recognised.

Close inspection of the first photograph in the light of the seemingly 'casual form' of the snapshot reveals clear signs of its 'documentary form'. Jack Hills, bluff and uncomplicated, faces the camera directly with relaxed good humour. Stella Duckworth stands detached, and slightly behind, her tense posture clearly at odds with that of her fiancé. She glances obliquely at the camera with a guarded, quizzical expression that suggests a wish to control and supervise the image-making. 'I'm watching you watching us,' she seems to say. In this photograph, Stella clearly enacts both of the roles discussed earlier: the modest fiancée and the supervisory mother figure.

If this first snapshot confirms Virginia's perception of the conflicting roles played by Stella on the visit, the second clearly captures that sense of exclusion which is a feature of her Bognor journal. It shows a couple walking arm-in-arm, at some distance, and walking away from the photographer. The picture, blurred as it is, clearly subverts the norms of the snapshot genre: we cannot see the subjects' faces; the subjects are moving; and they are some distance away from us. In this remarkable image we see an engaged couple literally walking out of the young photographer's life.

So far we have seen that the seemingly straightforward written and photographic records of Virginia's winter holiday

The same couple, walking away from the camera.

trace and explore patterns of tension and behaviour within the family group. When we turn to her third method of imposing shape and order on her experiences – reading – we will gain insights into quite a different aspect of her life: Virginia's apprenticeship as a writer. Reading was of central importance to her intellectual, artistic and emotional development. She chose holiday reading with great care and purpose. In a journal of August 1899 she compares herself as a reader to a Norse voyager frozen in the drift ice:

> The Seals and Walruses that I shoot during my excursions on the ice . . . are the books that I discover here and read. . . . There are worse situations than drift ice, and yet this eternal throbbing heart and energy of one's mind thaws a pathway thro'; and open sea and land shall come in time.

Such wintry metaphors are equally appropriate to her reading at Bognor in February 1897. Virginia's substantial reading on this holiday falls into two clear sections: her own choice of volumes four and five of John Lockhart's *Life* which she brought with her; and Stella's choice of W.E. Norris's *A Deplorable Affair* (1892), supplemented by readings aloud by her from Norris's earlier novel, *Madame de Mersac* (1883).

A Deplorable Affair, which Virginia began and finished on Monday 8 February, is an urbane, plot-driven novel. The action revolves around the library and reading rooms of a Bognor-like setting which Norris describes as 'not one of the most important watering-places on the South Coast, nor are we largely patronised either by the aristocracy or by cheap trippers'. The heroine, Beatrice Devereux, is a professional writer of children's books and often discusses the publishing trade with the fussy, inquisitive owner of the library, Mr Sykes, by whom the action of the novel is narrated. The plot hinges on a fraud perpetrated by the heroine's brother, who disguises himself as Beatrice to acquire jewels entrusted to her care. In sharp contrast to the Bognor-like setting of *A Deplorable Affair*, the action of Norris's earlier *Madame de Mersac* takes place in North Africa where 'the season was the month of

February and Northern Europe was still hard frozen or dreary with gales and driving rain, though here in Algeria the roses were in bloom and the air was full of the scent of spring'. Ironically, for the visit to Bognor, the central theme of this novel is the long, drawn-out engagement of the heroine Jeanne de Mersac and her lover St Luc. Furthermore, several key incidents in the novel hinge on the concept of chaperonage.

The importance of Virginia's immersion in the novels of W.E. Norris at Bognor is twofold. First, they were the subject of some of her earliest reviews when she became a professional writer. Second, and of much greater significance, it is clear that, through her early critical reading of Norris, she began to define and formulate her own views of a very different form of novel. Thus, in a review of Norris's *Barham of Beltana* on 17 March 1905, she writes that 'he tells his simple story without any desire to discuss problems or suggest that every thing is not precisely as it ought to be' (McNeillie, 1986). Again, reviewing Norris's *Lone Marie* on 1 November 1905, she contrasts him unfavourably with Henry James, noting that although 'there is the same economy of incident and restraint of treatment and even a trace of Mr James's marvellous penetration . . . the fact is he is ready to stop when Mr James is just ready to begin'. Virginia's rejection of Norris's superficial approach to character and experience, encountered in her reading at Bognor, represented a small step towards the later development of her own novels, which, by contrast, would 'let us record the atoms as they fall upon the mind in the order in which they fall, let us trace the pattern, however disconnected in appearance which each sight or incident scores upon the consciousness' (McNeillie, 1988).

If Norris's *A Deplorable Affair* gave some glimpses into the life of a professional writer, Virginia's other reading at Bognor – John Lockhart's *Life* – provided a detailed, extensive account of the profession of writing on an altogether grander scale. The work is a masterpiece of the biographer's art. Little wonder that Virginia referred in her journal to 'my beloved Lockhart'. Under his pen, the professional triumphs of Scott are unfolded like the battle honours of a literary Marlborough. The publication and acclaim of *Waverley*, *Guy Mannering*, *Old Mortality* and *Rob Roy* are chronicled with lively panache, together with the political and financial dramas which attended them. Scott emerges as an immensely likeable, humane, learned figure, equally at home with the victors of Waterloo, the aristocracy of Edinburgh, the literary coteries of London and his own domestic servants.

Having chronicled the public and literary achievements of Scott from 1812 to 1818, Lockhart brings volume five of his biography to triumphant conclusion with an extended celebration of the convivial social life of the novelist's literary circle. The centrepiece of this account consists of a detailed description of Scott's 'Sanctum', or writing room:

> The walls were entirely clothed with books; most of them folios and quartos all in that complete state of repair which at a glance reveals a tinge of bibliomania. . . . His own writing apparatus was a very handsome old box, richly carved, lined with crimson velvet. . . . Besides his own huge elbow chair, there were but two others in the room and one of these seemed, from its position, to be reserved exclusively for the amanuensis.
>
> (Lockhart, 1839, vol. 5, p. 321)

Lockhart's description of what he calls Scott's 'den' clearly confirmed the need for a professional writer to have 'a room of one's own'.

Virginia concluded her 1897 journal, which included the five days spent at Bognor, with the comment: 'Here is a volume of fairly acute life (the first really lived year of my life) locked and put away.' Even the five unhappy days at Bognor, seemingly dismissed by Virginia with an ironic journal comment ('So goodbye to that beloved Bognor!'), comprised much 'fairly acute life', which was shaped and interpreted in the three media that have been examined. The journal, a seemingly factual record, shapes the experience by its covert emphasis on emotional exclusion. The photographs confirm and record the familial tensions and conflicts within the visiting party in images that, for all their *naïveté* of execution, clearly signal a documentary intention. Finally, the pattern of Virginia's reading at Bognor indicates her continuing and active apprenticeship as a writer. The novels of W.E. Norris, which she was soon to review, provided her with early examples of the superficialities and limitations of the popular novel of manners. Lockhart's *Life*, on the other hand, provided a rich account of the summits of achievement open to those who seek out and pursue the profession of letters. The journal of 1897 may have been 'ended locked and put away', but the events that it chronicles, including the visit to Bognor, were clearly not, and were to influence and help shape her development as a woman and a writer.

FAIRY TALE

Alison MacLeod

In a certain kingdom near the sea, where there are hills of flint
and straw fields that glow like molten gold in the afternoon
light, there once lived a beautiful girl; a miller's daughter who
was both shrewd and clever. So the story goes. There lived also
a little man to whom she was greatly indebted; a stranger who
would one day demand an exacting price – unless she could
discover his name.

And if she never did? Another story.

The young queen (for she had married well) lay awake all
night, thinking of all the names she had ever heard, and
dispatched messengers all over the land to inquire after new
ones. She began with Timothy, Benjamin, Jeremiah and all the
names she could remember; but to all of them he only said,
'That's not my name.' Bandy-legs, she tried. Hunchback.
Crookshanks. But the little gentleman still said to every one of
them: 'That's not my name.'

> BABY FOUND ON DOWNS
> HANDS TIED TOGETHER –
> PRACTICALLY NAKED

'What will you give me to spin gold for you this time?' he
had said.

'I have nothing left'.

'Then promise me your first little child.'

What was she? A shrewd and clever girl? A queen who could
command anything? A woman who could spin herself a tale to
believe in like gold out of straw? She promised.

But later, would she discover his name?

> PINIONED BABE IN THE THICKET

August 26 1937. '**A baby girl, practically naked and with her hands tied together, was found on the Downs near Sompting on Thursday evening.**'

In the emergency ward in Worthing, the sisters prised thorns from her flesh with tweezers. They wiped the insect bites and scratches with cotton wool and witch hazel. They rubbed her feet and hands. They weighed her; measured her. They shone a small torch in her eyes. They marvelled at how well nourished and clean she had evidently been before she was abandoned. Her nails were clipped. There was no trace of that summer's hot sun on her face. She still smelled of talcum. The sisters recorded her age as twelve months. Already heavy to pick up.

It couldn't have been an easy spot to get to, up that sliding hillface, through a yew wood clotted with roots and blackberry bushes. A pram would have been impossible.

('Somebody must have had me in their arms.' Sixty years ago. A lifetime away. In a certain kingdom.)

At the birth of her first little child the queen forgot the little man and her promise; but one day he came into her chamber and reminded her of it. Then she offered him all the treasures of the kingdom in exchange, but in vain. At last, though, her tears softened him, and he said: 'I will give you three days' grace, and if during that time you tell me my name, you shall keep your child.'

Who was he? A stranger. An outsider. A man who lived alone on top of a high hill, under the wheeling crows, among the trees of the forest, whose name was not known to any census. A man who could spin gold, yet demanded a young woman's possessions: a necklace, a ring – her child. Sheer spite, or an old man's longings?

'**Bloodhounds assisted the police yesterday in a search on the South Downs for the person who abandoned a 12-month-old baby girl in a thicket, naked and with hands tied behind her. The search had not succeeded late last night.**' The dogs had traced the trail as far as Lancing Station, then lost the scent.

What is the scent of a fairy-tale mother? Does she bathe in ewe's milk? Does she dab her ears and throat with myrrh?

(What would you say to her now? Sixty years on. A lifetime away. I would say: 'I love you.')

The police treated the incident as attempted murder.

'They hadn't got the guts to kill her,' said one eyewitness. 'And they thought that's what they'd do, so they left her there tied up, so she couldn't move.'

There are stories, aren't there. Baby Moses buoyant among the bulrushes. *The Perils of Pauline.* The newborn babe the fairies steal. The little one that the angels have carried away. There are no stories that tell of children smothered in their sleep; flushed down loos; left naked and bound in a wood.

Her picture was flashed all over the world. A good head of hair. Fierce eyes.

On the Wednesday, he had watched her coming, her shoulders stooped by the weight tied to her chest. She had waited till the sun had started to drop in the sky; then the farmhands had gone in for the day. Then she'd skirted the edges of the fields, picking her way through the flint rubble; starting at the suddenness of scarecrows, their tin-lid eyes glinting in the last of the day's light.

For a time, he'd lost sight of her as she disappeared into a seam of black yews. As she'd walked, she'd counted the days to her daughter's birthday. Twelve. She'd thought of the cake they were to have: white with a single candle. She'd fingered the spot where she knew the little birthmark was, under the fleece blanket, on her right hip, a patch of skin the colour of clay, like the one on her own hip. When the child had started to cry, she'd stopped short, remembering a bottle of ear drops on a nursery table, like a detail in a dream.

When she'd emerged at last from the wood at the top of the hill, she saw a low fire burning and, next to it, the shape of the little man, stunted as a tree that has grown in the wind. A face rough as pine bark. A crack of a mouth. What had made her promise?

She was a beautiful girl, exceedingly shrewd and clever.

Yet one word from this little man and her story would unravel: her marriage to the king, her father's easy retirement, her kingdom, her touch-of-gold fingers.

She had passed him the child; smelled the musky stench of sweat, fungus and fox in his clothes; watched the colour rise in his face as he stroked her daughter's yellow hair. The wind was keening in the yew trees now. She thought about the steep descent in the encroaching dark, but didn't move. She watched his back disappear over the sharp rise of the hill, and still didn't move. She stood there, for she didn't know how long, as if she'd been turned to stone.

He had never held a child before. He had never held another person next to him. He removed her clothes and buried them, so that she'd never find them, so that she'd never ask. The night was warm. He looked around for a place in which to lay her; settled on the cradle of a blackberry bush. She cried and wriggled as he laid her down. 'There, there,' he said, and he turned her onto her belly so that she wouldn't roll in the night. He pulled the cord from round his waist and tied her wrists behind her to try to still her worried limbs. There, there.

He plucked ripening berries from the tree and tried to feed her. 'Sssh,' he whispered, pressing his cheek next to hers, 'my name is Rumplestiltskin.' He could feel her breath on his face, and it warmed him.

Her knees were stiff with cold as she descended, awkwardly. Light was already splitting the darkness, and overhead she could hear the crows cawing. Despite herself, she remembered: the golden motes of grain on the air; the stone walls of her father's mill, cold and sweaty to the touch. Outside, the warmth of April; lambs in the fields. She had wandered out; sneezed with the dust from the mill in her nose. There was the voice of her father saying: 'Only as far as the pasture wall.' The flap of black wings in the near distance.

Then just over the wall, the ripped body of a lamb, and four crows feeding on it.

The farmer had told her that they'd pecked out its eyes first, to blind it to their movements. 'They're canny,' he said. Then they'd pulled at the thread of its birth cord, unstitching the seam of its gut, eating it alive.

There are stories, aren't there. Later, she would tell her husband, the king, that a little man had stolen their child in the night; that they would never find him for no one in all the land knew him; that she would give him another. And he would believe her tale, for she had once spun gold out of straw.

FANTASIA ON TARRANT STREET: GEORGE MACDONALD IN ARUNDEL

William Gray

Between the River Arun and the hill crowned with Arundel Cathedral runs Tarrant Street. On a hot Sunday afternoon in July it seems narrow, surprisingly busy, and alive with unexpected sights and smells. Although Tarrant Street is still in some sense a working street, nowadays it is the tourist trade which dominates, and the pavement is lined with bistros, tearooms and antique shops. Set back from the street stands the Tarrant Street Antique Centre, advertised as Nineveh House, although it is actually the former Congregational chapel which was built on the site of the original and much less respectable house called Nineveh. It is an imposing if rather plain building, especially in comparison with the Romantic fantasy architecture which dominates Arundel. The interior of the church has been reconstructed to allow a collection of antique shops to display their wares: books, pictures, mirrors, old army uniforms, porcelain, brass and various kinds of furniture. One is lured from level to level of the building (there is a gallery and a cellar as well as the ground floor), browsing among the great variety of objects on sale.

Particularly interesting to anyone who happens to know something about Tarrant Street's most famous resident is the number of curious wardrobes and suspiciously unassuming writing desks on display. For you never know when a wardrobe is going to take you into another country, or when a secret compartment in a writing desk will open to reveal a visitor from Fairyland with an alarming propensity to grow from six inches to six feet in an instant, just to make a philosophical point. C.S. Lewis's discovery that another country is always just around the corner, or maybe through a wardrobe, was by his own admission decisively influenced by the inhabitant of 48 Tarrant Street in the early 1850s, a young poet from the north of Scotland, George MacDonald.

MacDonald was the minister of Trinity Congregational Church, Tarrant Street, from 1850 until he was forced to resign in 1853 because of his unorthodox theological views (he believed, it seems, that some animals and perhaps even the heathen had a chance of getting to heaven) and because of his temerity in translating into English some hymns by one of the greatest of the German Romantic poets (all things German, and especially ideas, were, of course, deeply suspect).

MacDonald's stay at Arundel was relatively brief, and he was never to repeat the experience of being a pastoral minister, though he did become a celebrated preacher. Instead he was for the rest of his life to earn his living by his pen. In 1858 he published his first prose work, *Phantastes: A Faerie Romance*, which so influenced C.S. Lewis, and in whose first chapter we meet the rather alarming fairy in the writing desk. Particularly in his fantasy writing, both for adults and for children (his most famous children's book is *The Princess and the Goblin*), MacDonald shows himself acutely aware that what we call 'reality' is only a temporary and ultimately unstable attempt to fix the free play of the imagination, and to exclude the magic of poetry which creates our world in the first place. In this he was deeply influenced by the German poet and thinker Novalis, some of whose poems he translated and had printed in Arundel for Christmas 1851.

MacDonald's refusal to give the last word to 'this world', and the disconcerting ease with which he can pass into another world, were not only a legacy to C.S. Lewis; they were also shared with C.L. Dodgson (alias Lewis Caroll), whose *Alice in Wonderland*, published in 1865, was first tried out in 1862 in manuscript form on the MacDonald children, to a hugely enthusiastic reception. But these convictions largely came to MacDonald from Novalis, one of whose fragments provides the epigraph for the last chapter of *Phantastes*, as well as being one of MacDonald's favourite and most often-used quotations:

'Our life is no dream; but it ought to become one, and perhaps will.' George MacDonald's life in Arundel was no dream, though whether Arundel itself was to become one, and what MacDonald would make of it, remains to be seen.

The young poet and pastor who moved in 1851 into 48 Tarrant Street, and whose first children were born there, was born in 1824 in Huntly, Aberdeenshire, of Highland stock. His background was not wealthy, but following the Scottish tradition where higher education was never the prerogative of the rich, he went at sixteen years old to Aberdeen University, where he won a bursary. He was an able if not always diligent student, doing well in natural science and languages. His acquisition of German at this time was to open to him the riches of German literature and thought, even if years later his congregation at Arundel would not share his enthusiasm for German culture. A crucial experience in his student years was the time spent 'in a certain castle or mansion in the North . . . cataloguing a neglected library'. It was here that he was able to widen his knowledge of literature, and especially German Romantic literature. He also fell in love with one of the young ladies of the castle, who, it seems, rejected him because of the difference in social class. This unhappy experience appears to have left its mark on him. The power and dominance of the gentry in 'the big house' would, of course, have been even more strikingly apparent in Arundel, though ironically it was with the narrow-minded conservatism of the nonconformist shopkeepers, many of whom would have had premises along Tarrant Street, that MacDonald was to tangle.

On completing his degree at Aberdeen University, MacDonald made the long journey south to London, where, after working for three years as private tutor to a wealthy family, he enrolled, in 1848, at Highbury College, a Congregational Theological Hall, to train for the pastoral ministry. In London he quickly acquired a new circle of friends, centring on the Powells in Clapton, to whom he was introduced by his cousin Helen MacKay, who had married one of the sons, and with whom

MacDonald had been very close – perhaps even romantically involved. It was Louisa Powell, however, to whom MacDonald paid suit, and when the Powells took a house in Brighton for August and September 1850, MacDonald undertook supply preaching in the Congregational Church in Arundel, which was conveniently near. The congregation took to him, and it soon became clear that he would be invited to become minister. Although he was approached by a wealthier and more fashionable church in Brighton, MacDonald decided to accept the call to Arundel. He was obviously drawn to this 'very quiet little town' (it is not only MacDonald who remarked on the lack of bustle in Arundel at this time) and its people, although he had illusions about neither. Writing home to a younger relative, he offers this attractive sketch of Arundel (without allowing a moment's doubt as to his abiding loyalty to Old Scotia):

> Behind the town there are very low hills, with sweet short grass, on which numbers of fallow deer are feeding. Here and there are plantations of very fine trees, and down in one of the hollows rises and runs a stream of water, clearer than the Bogie, and so nice to drink in the hot days. . . . We have a river that runs through the town, up which vessels come of a good size, bringing things and taking away things; but it is a very quiet little town – not so much bustle as Huntly. . . . The fields grow much richer crops than with you, and there are many more trees growing about the fields; but it is not such a beautiful country to my mind, nearly, as the one I left.
>
> (Grenville MacDonald, p. 137)

His admiration of the people is also qualified:

> The people are a simple people – not particularly well informed – mostly tradespeople – and in middling circumstances. They chiefly reside in the town, which has between two and three thousand inhabitants. There are none I could call society for me – but with my books now and the beautiful earth, and added to these soon, I hope, my wife – and above all that, God to care for me – in whom I and all things are – I do not much fear the want of congenial society.

With hindsight we can perhaps wonder whether books could ever have been a substitute for 'congenial society', particularly when the atmosphere of the books differs so sharply from that of sleepy little Arundel (and especially if the books were as esoteric as the ones mentioned in *Annals of a Quiet Neighbourhood*, MacDonald's fictionalized version of his Arundel years).

In October 1850, George MacDonald accepted the invitation to be minister of Trinity Congregational Church, Tarrant Street, for an annual stipend of £150. However, the ordination service, planned for the following month, had to be postponed because in early November MacDonald was taken ill with haemorrhaging of the lungs. This was his first serious attack of the lung disease that was to plague his life, and that of his family, taking loved ones to an early grave with distressing regularity. Whatever may be the ultimate origins of that note of bleakness and despair which runs through MacDonald's work, and the accompanying nostalgia for another world, the experience of disease and loss affected him deeply, as it did Novalis, whose poems he must have been translating during this period. And whatever the literary merits of MacDonald's translation of Novalis's 'Spiritual Song' no. 13 (no. 12 in MacDonald's Arundel version, which reduced Novalis's cycle of fifteen poems to twelve), there can be little doubt of the immediacy, the intensity and the authenticity of the feelings involved:

> When in hours of fear and weakness,
> Our poor heart almost despairs,
> When, o'erwhelmed with its sickness,
> Anguish at our spirit tears;
> Thinking of the true-loved pining,
> All their troubles rise to view,
> And the clouds our gaze confining
> Not a beam of hope looks through.
> O, then God doth bend him tow'rd us,
> His love to us cometh near;
> Long we then to pass the borders,
> Stands his angel by us here.

Of fresh life he brings to chalice,
Whispers courage to our breast;
Nor in vain, from the dark valleys,
For the loved we pray for rest.

MacDonald went to convalesce on the Isle of Wight. The invalid was not idle, however, and during his convalescence he composed the dramatic poem 'Within and without', which was to make his name in the literary world when published in 1855. He resumed his pastoral duties in Arundel on 16 January 1851, and prior to his marriage to Louisa Powell on 8 March he moved into 48 Tarrant Street, the rent and furnishings for which were provided by MacDonald's prospective father-in-law.

While Arundel enjoyed its golden period in the latter part of the eighteenth century, when it is said briefly to have rivalled Brighton with its social season, by the mid-nineteenth century the town was more noted, it seems, for its sleepiness. There is a little guide called *A Day in Arundel*, by one George Hillier, published in 1847 by Mitchell and Son, High Street, Arundel, incidentally the same firm that was to print MacDonald's Novalis translations in 1851, and that published the first edition of *The West Sussex Gazette* on 1 June 1853, just days after MacDonald had resigned his charge in Arundel at the end of May 1853. It is conceivable that MacDonald might have acquired the guide, as a newcomer, to introduce himself to Arundel. In it he would have read:

> The present description of the Town is, that it is one of quietness and absence of bustle in the streets, the houses mostly unpretending, with none of those gay resuscitations and extensions which mark the modern growth of most towns perceptible; on market days it awakens a little from its apparent somnolent condition, which appearance is observable every alternate Monday.

However, it is difficult altogether to believe in this remarkable absence of bustle in Arundel if one consults contemporary records, for there are recorded a relatively large number and variety of traders with addresses in Tarrant Street. At any rate, the writer of *A Day in Arundel* thinks that in Tarrant Street 'little is observable either of interest or antiquity' apart from a house with a fifteenth-century arched doorway that was 'a place of assemblage of the Quakers, at the period of the severe and unmerited persecution they underwent'. This house was demolished in about 1900, although there survives a photograph of it, looking for all the world like a magic doorway in a MacDonald fantasy novel. The name 'Tarrant' derives, the guide tells us, from *Tarent*, the Saxon name for the river now called Arun. There is only one other feature worthy of mention, according to Hillier, as we move along Tarrant Street, apart from the turrets and rugged, ivy-clad keep of the castle which towers over the houses, and which, of course, is different from the present castle, the latter having been substantially rebuilt between 1890 and 1903 (the Cathedral was not built until 1870). This feature is the 'edifice, in the Norman style, of some architectural pretensions' which claims 'at least passing notice' because of its being erected on the site of 'an ancient hostelrie, known as Nineveh, which bore the date of 1440'. Of the history of Nineveh nothing can be known 'save conjecture', says Hillier. Although later historians of Arundel agree that some mystery surrounds the origins and history of the building known as Nineveh, it was probably erected between 1415 and 1422. By 1440 it was a hostelry, later known as The Star, and by 1650 it had become a tenement for labourers, which it remained until its demolition in 1833. No one knows how Nineveh acquired its exotic name. It seems, however, to have been a substantial building, with spacious and beautifully decorated rooms. The great mantelpiece in particular has been described as being 'of the greatest beauty and elegance'. Between the house and the river, in the area later occupied by Nineveh Shipyard, now derelict but still visible from the riverbank, lay Nineveh's 'pleasure grounds'. One suspects that the enthusiasm with which the marvels of Nineveh are described by several writers may owe something to the 'cavaliers versus roundheads' attitude. The exotic and glamorous Nineveh was, after all, replaced in 1836 by the sober and imposing Congregational Chapel. It therefore seems ironic but also curiously fitting that the young Highlander ordained minister of Tarrant Street Congregational Church in 1851 should himself have been rather exotic, with a taste for German mysticism and fantasy literature, and for outrageous waistcoats (George MacDonald was all his life something of a dandy). And where else would a wardrobe in Tarrant Street Antique Centre lead but back to Nineveh?

Nineveh at any rate has had the last word, since the chapel built to replace it is now called Nineveh House. The building, however, to those who were brought up in the Congregational tradition (and no doubt others) has been unable entirely to shake off the atmosphere of worship. Boredom (and the present writer had better say he is speaking only from personal experience: any resemblance to any church service, living or dead, is purely coincidental) seems ingrained in the windows, whose little red and yellow triangles must have been repeatedly counted during endless sermons and (but who could admit to having their eyes open to detect the culprits?) endless prayers. Even Mrs MacDonald did not always turn out to hear the visiting preacher's sermon, while George was spreading the Word in Worthing, Brighton or Chichester. One visitor's sermon contained twenty-five headings, though fortunately, her son records, Louisa MacDonald was down the street at number 48, seeing to Sunday dinner.

What is particularly striking about the stained-glass windows of the Tarrant Street Chapel are the swallows in the roundels at the centre of each of the three windows facing the street. A reproduction of the roundel has been set on top of the main sign for Nineveh House on Tarrant Street. And as you come out of the main entrance to the chapel and look north, you can make out, perched on the roof of the Town Hall, a giant seven-foot bright-blue swallow, echoing (parroting? Apologies to Julian Barnes, but Flaubert would have relished the tale of Arundel's giant swallows) the one in the sign and in the windows. The swallow as an emblem of Arundel goes back to medieval times; some would even derive the town's name from the French *hirondelle*. The swallow stands on top of Arundel's coat of arms,

Detail from a window at Tarrant Street Congregational Chapel (Ninevah House), Arundel.

but only in more recent times has it appeared on top of the Town Hall. A giant wooden swallow had originally graced the Swallow Brewery just across the river, and had been donated to the town when the brewery closed. But after seventy years this swallow was beginning to show its age; candidly, it was starting to rot. To the rescue came a somewhat eccentric gentleman who volunteered to replace the rotting town swallow with a brand-new, fibreglass bird, which he subsequently, it seems, became attached to, and reluctant to part with. Only after his death did the town finally acquire the bright blue swallow, now perched in all its seven-foot splendour on the roof of the Town Hall. Some locals have found the new bird a little hard to accept, principally on account of its almost fluorescent blue colour, but also because of the unnatural substance out of which it has been created; rumour has it that on occasion it has even been referred to in gentle, no doubt affectionate, banter as the 'plastic pigeon'. Be that as it may, the swallow certainly forms a visual link between the Town Hall and Nineveh House, other than the Norman architecture, which apparently was all the rage in 1836. It's just that everything at the Town Hall is on a grander scale.

Although the present Town Hall was built in 1836, the borough of Arundel goes back to the thirteenth century, and a charter was obtained from Elizabeth I in 1586. Council meetings began to be minuted in 1539, and in the first minute book can be found the so-called 'Burgess's Oath', which contains the following admonition: 'Ye shall utterly avoyde backebytynge, sclawnderyng or tale-berynge.' MacDonald might well have wished that some of the members of his congregation had heeded the 'Burgess's Oath', for in 1852 began a determined campaign by a section of his congregation to make his position untenable. It has to be borne in mind that the ejection of a minister is a much less unusual affair in the Congregational tradition than it is in the Established Church. In the former tradition the local congregation has the complete power to appoint and dismiss its minister. This more democratic form of church government obviously has certain advantages when the minister is an inadequate or unpopular appointment; on the other hand, the abuse of power can occur here too. MacDonald complained in a letter to his father about being at the mercy of a group of tradesmen who 'regard you more as their servant than as Christ's'. It is significant that, ultimately, MacDonald was to leave the Congregationalists for the 'Broad' Church of England, and that the hero of his autobiographical novel set in Arundel (which gets renamed 'Marshmallows' in the novel, perhaps on account of the profusion of marshmallows which are still to be seen from the bridge by the mill) is a Church of England vicar. MacDonald's predecessors at Tarrant Street Chapel had hardly lasted longer than he was to.

Although the opposition to MacDonald focused on the question of his orthodoxy, it seems that, as in most theological disputes, there were other, less disinterested motives at work. As MacDonald's son puts it: 'these [criticisms of MacDonald's orthodoxy] were curiously coincident with the discovery that his residence, rented from the most influential of the deacons, was not large enough for his needs'. And MacDonald, through a mixture of boldness and naïvety, was never one to tailor his preaching to the sensitivities of the well-off, writing on one occasion: 'Riches indubitably favour stupidity', and on another telling the congregation of the wealthiest and most fashionable church in Glasgow: 'One may readily conclude how poorly God thinks of riches when we see the sort of people he sends them to!' There was also the consideration that, since his succumbing to lung disease, MacDonald could only preach for about twenty minutes, instead of the usual hour or more, so quite apart from the content of his sermons, some of his congregation may have felt (incredible to relate) short-changed by their relative brevity. And then there really was the question of their theological content. MacDonald had a mind which was constitutionally averse to any kind of dogmatism. As he wrote to his father from Arundel in April 1851:

> I firmly believe people have hitherto been a great deal too much taken up about doctrine and far too little about practice. The word *doctrine*, as used in the Bible, means teaching of duty, not theory. I preached a sermon about this. We are far too anxious to be definite and to have finished, well-polished, sharp-edged *systems* – forgetting that the more perfect a theory about the infinite, the surer it is to be wrong, the more impossible is it to be right. I am neither Armenian nor Calvinist. To no system would I subscribe. . . .

Apart from a reaction to the Calvinism he grew up with, we can also see here the influence of the German Romantics and especially of Novalis, who wrote, for example: 'Every true book is a Bible when the spirit gives its blessing.'

Suspicion of German thought was in the air. In 1846, Mary Ann Evans (alias George Eliot) had published a translation of David Friedrich Strauss's *The Life of Jesus*, which applied the 'myth theory' to the life of Christ, and which led to Strauss's dismissal from his academic post (he was never to secure another). And although Eliot's translation of Feuerbach's even more radical *The Essence of Christianity* was not to appear until 1854, awareness of the implications of German scholarship was spreading, especially perhaps in more educated nonconformist circles. By 1852 the word would have filtered through even to Arundel, even if only as rumour. So apart from MacDonald's views that possibly animals and – much worse – even the heathen might have some kind of afterlife (which must have sounded to Arundel's Protestants suspiciously like the papist doctrine of purgatory), there was the fact that MacDonald had had the local printer Mitchell and Son print copies of *Twelve of the Spiritual Songs of Novalis done into English by George MacDonald*, dated Christmas Day 1851. Had the deacons of Tarrant Street Chapel only known it, MacDonald had removed from his version of Novalis's *Geistliche Lieder* three of the songs which might actually have caused offence, and which MacDonald did include in his later version in his collection of poem translations entitled *Exotics*, published in 1876. The last two of Novalis's *Geistliche Lieder* are quite explicitly hymns to Mary, and might well have offended Protestant sensibilities in nineteenth-century Arundel. Number 7 of the original is also omitted; it is a highly charged mystical/erotic meditation on the Eucharist, in the tradition of the mystical interpretation of the Song of Solomon. No doubt its frank eroticism and its suggestions of transubstantiation would have made it dangerous for the minister of Tarrant Street Chapel to publish. But despite having in a sense bowdlerized Novalis, one of the charges brought against MacDonald by the deputation of deacons who visited 48 Tarrant Street towards the end of June 1852 was that he was 'tainted with German theology'.

There was also the accusation that he had stated from the pulpit: 'that with the Heathen the time of trial does not (in his, the Revd G. MacDonald's opinion) cease at their death'. The latter quotation is taken from the official record of 'a Meeting of the Church of Christ assembling in Trinity Chapel, Arundel, held July 5th 1852'. This meeting had been requested by MacDonald because he wanted the question of his orthodoxy, and of whether he should resign, to be discussed by the whole congregation, and not just by the group of deacons who had appeared on his doorstep in late June with the announcement that, since he was contemplating a larger house, his stipend must be unnecessarily generous and therefore in need of reduction. MacDonald had responded to this imposition of a pay cut of twenty-five per cent with: 'I am sorry enough to hear it, but if it must be, why, I suppose we must contrive to live on less.' What Louisa said is not recorded, but one can imagine that George's noble following of the Master's admonition to 'consider the lilies of the field' might have been rather trying for a young woman soon to fall pregnant with her second child. Certainly her father was displeased, but her sister Carrie came to Tarrant Street as a paying guest, and Louisa came up with the idea – abortive in the event – of starting a school. The MacDonalds did have friends in the congregation, however, who helped them with hand-outs of food; and Old Rogers, later to appear in *Annals of a Quiet Neighbourhood*, came with a gift of golden gooseberries. There is even a donation of some home-brewed beer, 'very strong and good for nursing'. However, the situation clearly could not last. MacDonald resigned his charge of Tarrant Street Congregational Church in May 1853. Louisa remained in number 48 awaiting the birth of their second child in July, while George set off to start a new life in a city which was in many respects the antithesis of Arundel – Manchester. He was, for the moment at least, leaving 'the warm, rich, indolent South' for 'the dear, rugged North'.

George MacDonald's life in Arundel was not a dream, though at times it must have seemed like a nightmare. More especially, Tarrant Street must have evoked very mixed feelings in him, with at one end the church of which he must at the age of twenty-six have been proud to be minister, and at the other his first home. Yet it all turned sour, and during his time at Arundel he must have been relieved to leave the street and take off into the surrounding district. MacDonald was a great walker, and when you read Hillier's *A Day in Arundel* (1847), particularly the sections describing his walk through the woods to and from the Black Rabbit ('a house of rural retirement and public entertainment') by way of the mill, ending up by the old bridge at the bottom of the High Street, there are strong echoes of *Annals of a Quiet Neighbourhood* and even, in the following passage, of Anodos's wanderings through the woods of fairyland in *Phantastes*:

> As we advance, the wood of beeches thickens, and the majesty of unassisted nature is beheld in its sloward, silent workings; many of the trunks being of immense size, the axe of the woodman not having been heard among them for many generations; the dry branch crackling beneath the tread, giving forth a hollow sound in the dead silence, until we come to where the lofty trees have been blown aside and slanting by the winds, the sunlight glancing among the leaves which overshadow the placid and translucent waters beneath, and dancing brightly on them; a graceful swan arching its stately neck, and sailing down the smooth stream.

In this sense, MacDonald's life at Arundel may have been turned into a dream, or a fiction. But Arundel itself, already a tourist attraction in the early nineteenth century, was increasingly to become a figment of the imagination. As a 'real' place its existence has become ever more questionable as the town becomes ever more a simulacrum, a Romantic fantasy, which exists only in the minds of its visitors. And as the fairy-tales collected (or perhaps 'packaged') by the brothers Grimm in the Romantic period, and imitated by the likes of Novalis and, following him, George MacDonald, were to end up as part of the Disney industry, so Arundel, with its long history, was by the end of the nineteenth century largely a fake, a copy, a show. The past has become a lucrative commodity. Current intellectual fashion would ridicule those who imagine it might be otherwise. None of this 'heritage industry' would surprise a Scot, especially one as fey and self-promoting as MacDonald could be. MacDonald had the nerve, one suspects, actually to believe that he was George MacDonald, to paraphrase Sartre on that other outsize Victorian beard, Victor Hugo. 'Nevertheless, nevertheless,' as Muriel Spark, another Scot writing south of the border, might say. It does seem a shame to end up with a plastic pigeon.

THREE POEMS

Vicki Feaver

[Vicki Feaver lives near Chichester, at West Ashling, and often visits the beach at the Witterings, where the horned poppy grows, and also Kingley Vale, where the great yews stand. The 'pond' is in her own village. Ed.]

Horned Poppy

Frailest of flowers, armoured
to survive at the sea's edge: leaves
tough like holly, hugging the stem
like spiked cuffs; the bud protected
by a prickly sheath; the petals furled
like yellow parachute silk, opening to expose,
at its radiant heart, the threads
of stamens, pollen's loose dust.
It blooms for at the most an hour;
torn apart by the elements it loves.
And then the pistil grows:
a live bootlace, a fuse
of multiplying cells – reaching out
to feel between the shingle's
sharp edged flints for a moist bed
to lay its seed; or in my kitchen,
drying in the heat, a long thin hand
summoning a salt gale, a tide to roll in
over the flat land, roaring
through the open door.

Yews

Fed on the blood of Vikings,
stained a deep umber red,
trees driven by the passion
of xylem and phloem
to break out of the fastness of wood,
twisting into tusks, necks, heads.
Trees that contradict the belief
in trees as good: poisoners,
their venom in feathery needles,
in seeds buried in the pulp
of the female's orange berries.
I stand in their smothering tents,
the space where nothing grows,
adjust to the thin light,
the resinous stillness,
the sleepiness of thinking:
this would be the moment
to lie down and die. They welcome me
with empty eyes.

Pond

Not deep enough for a drowning,
or even a baptism: murky, undredged.
I bring my sorrows and stale bread
to the mounting stone at its edge;
filling my lungs with its breath.
I test temperatures and surfaces:
water excited by the couplings
of clouds and willows, torn
by the flurries of webbed feet;
the swans' heat as they swoon
on the nest, their close packed plumage
not immaculate – a model for angels' wings –
but stained yellow at the feathers' tips;
a beak that could poke out an eye
in a fierce caress.

From 'Hills Beloved' to 'Fractured Cliff': The Landscape of Charlotte Smith

John Wyatt

'Why do you think winter is a woman?' you ask me. We are gazing down on the Roman mosaic floor of the Four Seasons at Bignor. Winter looks up at us, blue-grey with steady seen-it-all eyes. Her (his?) head is draped in a cloth the colour of a thunderstorm cloud, and folds envelop the neck and arms. He (she?) holds a woeful bare branch. I agree – it is an unnecessary presumption to give a woman the cold, dreary part and, having negotiated a settlement, we go out to sit on a bench in the August sun. Before us stretches the scarp slope of the South Downs. From its gently curved skyline hang deep-edged

Winter: *mosaic at Bignor Roman Villa.*

Charlotte Smith: 'strange Defeatures in my Face'.

shadows, the woods that gather on the steepest part of the slope. Below, the fields are ochre with the harvest. Two combine-harvesters are working half a mile away before us, turning their field into a dark umber across which drifts of dust blow, slowly dispersing into the immense circle of the clear sky. The higher rounded summits march across the vista – Duncton Down, Barlavington Down, West Burton Hill; and across the steep valley of the Arun, hidden now by the edge of Bury Hill, we can see the immense flower-like white scar of Amberley chalk quarry.

Winter's medallion of woe still concerns me. There is another reason (other than basic male presumption) that identifies the mosaic with woman. We are sauntering on from the Roman site this hot afternoon, with a mild purpose, to walk in Bignor Park, where Charlotte Smith, the novelist and poet, lived at the end of the eighteenth century. I realize that I have in my inner eye another medallion. It is of a sad woman, an engraving of Charlotte, published with her *Elegiac Sonnets* and the collection called *Beachy Head*. There she looks as downcast as the Roman image of winter. She, too, is enveloped, but in conventional wrappings of a matron – a huge bonnet with a large bow and a seemly-collared gown. She gazes sadly to her left, conscious of the victories life has gained over her. Beneath the portrait is engraved a quotation from Shakespeare's *Comedy of Errors* (V.i. 299 ff):

> Oh! Time has Changed me since you saw me last,
> And heavy Hours with Time's deforming Hand
> Have written strange Defeatures in my Face.

We progress a mile or two idly on to Bignor Park. Through the landscaped park is a private road, so we leave the car and walk on. Cattle shelter from the sun in the deep, dark grass around the neat copses of oaks and sycamores, for this is picturesque by intention. Like a number of large estates to the north and south of the chalk down, it is part of our inheritance. Wealthy landowners developed large (but not vulgarly large) houses and attendant farms on the spring-line that feeds from the rains falling on the Downs, which slowly and secretly percolate through the chalk. There are rich pastures, enough clay and marl, enough light soil in bands across the lower Greensand ridge. A good life was possible here. The Romans seemed to enjoy one, as did those who came to settle in Sussex from London and its eighteenth-century economic miracles.

Charlotte's family (the Turners) were well bottomed economically. She was married at the age of fifteen in 1765 into a wealthy family that had made its money in that rich picking-field, the East India Company. For many years, the best, Charlotte lived in Bignor Park. The worst was to follow, for Benjamin Smith, her husband, was a waster of his own money and of hers as well – but more of winter later.

This warm afternoon it is all August and there is no sensation of anything so bad taste as to be disorderly. In the deep woods that border the first mile of the road into the park, there are, if you look for them, clues of catastrophe: tall pines are tilted badly; roots of great trees lie like fallen great mushrooms. The 1987 gale still displays its devastation through the Sussex woods. In the soft, green parkland, groups of oaks gather together, undisturbed from the last century, but there are signs of a bad night in the great stumps, marked still by the chainsaw's cut. Nothing else can be seen now even to hint of chaos. A private tennis court has been created opposite the large house. Racquets and sweaters lie on the grass, their owners gone off for tea. A row of fully grown sunflowers are drilled in line against the great garden wall of Bignor Park House. Each plant is held in place with a piece of twine tied to a rail high on the wall. Here there is a calm, green prosperity. As we return to the public road, the only other people we have seen for an hour drive with discretion into the park.

It isn't long before we are into the traffic noise of the main road from London to the south coast; it grinds up Bury Hill and, for a brief, gently sloping moment, steals a breathless view of the Arun Valley with the sea shining in the distance beyond the edge of Arundel Park. Then our homeward journey is a longer, slower descent on the great dip-slope of the Downs down to the sea. I remember suddenly that this transect is doubly familiar, from so many journeys of recent years and from distant school lessons, for these are the classic south-east England eroded folds of chalk and sandstone, the massive Weald astrodome of curved strata to be demolished by the ages of Pliocene and Pleistocene like an ancient pot cracked open by water and frost. The outer limbs of the great up-turned chalk bowl remain, and within the time-rotted arena the strata beneath the chalk are revealed: gault clay, lower greensand and Wealden sands in successive, neat ordering. On the edges of the remnant of the dome are the London clay beds and thin strata of sandstones, covered by the mixed rubble of chalk, clay and flints washed down in millennia of storms and aeons of gales. Wild seasons unimaginable have made an edge to the North and South Downs with thick clay that forms the gentle, bumpy slope to the sea. Then finally the sea itself has added its ruff of new alluvium, stripping away the new to reveal the clay strata, its shoreline shifting with tides in a millennium cycle matching our diurnal shifting ebbs and flows. I have known this south-eastern landscape in theory as a boy and in practice as a man.

At school the cross-section was something to copy from a textbook, with dotted lines reaching into deep time below the surface and emerging the other side of the Channel in the Paris Basin through poppies and the torn alluvium, and the superficial scratches of trenches with their modern burdens of death. Each tilted layer, each stripe of landscape, was a scene in Charlotte's life, a slow decline from happiness to austerity, holding poverty at bay.

It is another day, early in summer, and we walk on Bury Hill. Within minutes the traffic roar has gone and the bird song has become dominant. It was at this point, as we dip down the chalk lane between the thin edge of new grass and early riots of bramble, that we saw two deer emerge from the deep dark of the wood. Another mile of walking and the path climbs steeply, so we can look down on the strange curved segments of the skyline, the full circle of a dew pond and the clouds' shadows moving over the new grain. I imagine the fields and edge of the deer wood at night and think how silent it must be, but for the owls. Then I remember the nightjar. Only a week ago, a friend who lives a mile or so from Bury greeted me hard on the heels of 'Good morning' with the welcoming invitation: 'We heard a nightjar again last night'. The bird appears in one of Charlotte's poems – but for her, as an omen of melancholy to come.

The chalk downs and serene Bignor to the north were her blissful years. The sonnets which praise the South Downs are nostalgic, occasions for regret at freedom lost, at careless youth flown too quickly.

> Ah! hills so early loved! in fancy still
> I breathe your pure keen air, and still behold
> Those widely spreading views, mocking alike
> The Poet and the Painter's utmost art.
>
> (*Beachy Head*)

I admit that there is convention here. Sadness was a mark of the sensitive soul of the time – of shy, frightened Gray sheltering in his Cambridge college; of poor, terrified Cowper, convinced of the depth of his iniquity. Melancholy had its ascendant when the *Elegiac Sonnets* were composed in 1784:

> Ah, what to me can those dear days restore,
> When scenes could charm that now I taste no more!
> (Sonnet XXXI; Written in Farm Wood,
> on the South Downs, May 1784)

Not all is fashion and convention. The remarkable feature of Charlotte's hymns to nature is that they are grounded in the reality of the soil and the weather. Her feet trod those open chalk hills. Her arms brushed aside the branches of the woodland that cling to the cup-like curves of the slopes. She bent below the branches of the dark green yew and beech. She climbed up to the chalk with flints left by the tundra climate of the fringe of the Arctic glacial sheet that covered the land to the north of what is now the Thames Valley. Charlotte Smith is one of the first true women explorers, albeit in her own small patch. She has knowledge of the flora and fauna of the Downs. They are not decked with the imaginary, conventional, pastoral growths that support the classical shepherd. They are the rare but real flowers such as orchids ('tufts of Alpine flowers'), the more common wood sorrel (in a footnote labelled 'Oxalis acetosella') and the *Anemone nemorosa* of the woodland shade. She noted also more contentious matter. The Downs and their history give rise to thoughts of transience. Her late collection, *Beachy Head*, contains evidence of wider historical reading. There are 'half obliterated mounds/And half fill'd trenches', remnants of 'the mail'd legions, under Claudius' (*Beachy Head*).

Older even than the first warlike settlers are the Downs themselves and their rocks and fossils. Strange findings were beginning to disturb the calmer view of the Earth's history. In 1740 labourers at Burton Park discovered 'the teeth and bones of an elephant' which may have come with the Roman legions, but some thinkers gave a more disturbing explanation, hinting at breathtakingly older antiquity. The poet notes that she saw similar specimens from the New World when she visited Paris. Her own observation of the surface of the South Downs is one.

> Of sea shells; with the pale calcareous soil
> Mingled, and seeming of resembling substance
> *(Beachy Head)*

Charlotte continues to probe the thought that her observation has stimulated. She has read a little but has not been satisfied with explanations to account for why shells can be found so far from the sea. Although familiar with 'the late theories of the earth', she has not studied them: perhaps Erasmus Darwin's footnotes to *Zoonomia* told her as much as she wanted to know about contemporary science.

Next to the southern slopes of the Downs is the territory of cosy villages and comfortable houses tucked along the spring-line, linked by wandering lanes or by the straighter roads of Roman or modern Britain. Eartham, near National Trust Slindon, is the next place to evoke Charlotte's ghost. Eartham woods are good walking country too. They are deep, well cared for and an afternoon's small adventure now. You can lunch at the pub in Eartham and gently stroll in the bridle paths. In late autumn, the richness of the earth manifests itself in the holding at Slindon that sells pumpkins. By the lane, along the wall, on the eaves of the single-storey farm building, are rows of great suns, each a swelling orange individual. More exotic squashes are lined up, carbuncled, striped, curved in scatters of colour on rough shelves in the yard. We buy our seasonal pumpkin and plan to make enough soup for a platoon. With the great orange football rolling on the floor of the car, a touch of winter begins to feel its way into our hearts as we travel home in the early dark. The pub has started to light the small electric candles on each table. The evening menu is being chalked up on the blackboard that now extends across the walls of one side of the bar, for this has a well known reputation for 'meals out'. There at the top is a literary reference – Hayley's menu. Hayley, the patron of Cowper, of

Romney and, most famously, of Blake, lived in Eartham and his reputation is alive and well – but, except for the few who read poetry, reduced to chalk and cheese.

Like Bignor Park, the Hayley house is largely rebuilt. It is now a prep. school. Again, a severe decline in cultural power, but at least consistent – from a privileged literary salon to a privileged education. The ghost of Hayley's cultured evenings will feel at ease, surrounded by books, but less so with the computers provided by special events organized by aspiring parents. Turret House in Felpham, six or so miles away, the seaside retreat of Hayley and his friends, is there only in name – a small gatehouse left, a mound (like that the Danes left on the Downs) and the garden that leads to the retirement flats that have been built in the grounds of the pleasure house.

No pleasure, but respite here for the established Charlotte Smith, emerging from her personal disasters with a significant reputation as a novelist, one of the best known of her generation. Not the Catherine Cookson of her time, but producing as many stories to entertain, to thrill and to cause a tear among the literate and those who went down to circulating libraries to borrow books. It was not the novel that brought her into the literary set surrounding Hayley and his guests but the more revered muse, poetry. For all her bestselling volumes of love betrayed and, eventually, love triumphant, Charlotte aimed for something higher. The prospect of a woman novelist was tenable, even fair to see, but a woman poet was an altogether less acceptable matter to the new breed of publisher–printers on the Strand who dominated the publishing world of the late eighteenth century.* Charlotte required powerful friends and, for a time, Hayley provided both patronage and friendship. In 1784 she dedicated her *Elegiac Sonnets* to him. He had allowed her to use his name after reading the poems sent from nearby Bignor Park:

*Nevertheless, the 1789 (5th) edition of the *Elegiac Sonnets* includes a list of subscribers extending to more than 800 names; and 47 per cent are women. Ed.

> Yet permit me to say that did I not trust your candour and sensibility, and hope they will plead for the errors your judgment must discover, I should never have availed myself of the liberty I have obtained – that of dedicating these simple effusions to the greatest modern Master of that charming talent, in which I can never be more than a distant copyist.

Feminine modesty in the extreme, but that was the way you had to operate then in order to operate at all. Perhaps she was not a regular member of Hayley's circle in those years. Biographers record that she was suddenly taken ill and given first aid at Eartham in 1784. What dramatic narrative is hidden here? Charlotte's heroines were given to having a bad turn, being overwhelmed by feeling and fainting away at crucial moments. Did Charlotte contrive an attack of sensibility? Did it occur at a good moment outside the house of a patron of the arts? We can only guess the worst.

There is a more enduring record. Hayley and his guests, William Cowper and George Romney, reported a substantial occasion in 1792 when Charlotte read to them from *The Old Manor House*, a novel which was then in preparation. A poem was dedicated to Cowper at this time and, with the newly published *The Old Manor House* and a new edition of *Elegiac Sonnets*, was sent to the shy poet; and Romney drew her portrait in crayons.

Then the charm of the Hayley house parties failed. Gradually, the correspondence from Charlotte reveals a cooling-off. Great men can display great condescension:

> In the days of our intimate friendship when I was the dear Muse, and had not stiffened into Sister of Parnassus or sunk into 'Poor Charlotte'; he used to laugh and say if I lived longest I should write his life and if he lived longest he would write mine. Tho this was mere badinage, I have since thought what work mine would make, for he could not praise me for Unwinian virtues.

(McKillop, p. 251)

Mrs Unwin was the comfortable, warm-hearted and essentially motherly protector of William Cowper. Without her tender care, poor Cowper would not have survived a week in the harsh world of every day. Charlotte was no soft pillow of a woman. 'Sister of Parnassus' indeed! That obviously hurt!

Brighton, where the Downs meet the sea, where the chalk rubble made a hard for boats and the beach a bathing place for princes. Brighton on a winter's Saturday afternoon. No bird song here, but the continuous sound of feet and the shingle, like voices. Students of language from the countries of the world collect their shopping in plastic bags emblazoned with the name of their language school. They wander in a happy, noisy daze, determinedly talking in their own language. Along the windswept promenade in this late winter sunlight, delegates to the international conference at the Brighton Centre lean against the wind and joke about English spring. The Prince Regent did well. He intended to recreate Kubla Khan's new citadel as the envy of the world. The pavilion eclectically grabbed the images of China, the decorations of India and the colours of the newly discovered South Seas. Now his town seizes the peoples of the world.

Standing on one of the high chalk clifftops that emerge from the sea's spray to the east of the town, a figure of poetry looks along the cliff edge. It is a narrator-poet from Charlotte's long poem, 'The Emigrants', part of which she read to Hayley and his guests.

> Slow in the wintry Morn, the struggling light
> Throws a faint gleam upon the troubled waves,
> Their foaming tops, as they approached the shore
> And the broad surf that never-ceasing brakes
> On the innumerable pebbles . . .

The scene is set for distress, but it is not nature's distress that the watcher on the cliff foresees. It is humanity's failure 'that mars God's work'. A group of displaced, homeless ones is seen across the cliff. They are emigrants from France. The watcher feels their sorrow:

> I mourn your sorrows; for I too have known
> Involuntary exile; and whilst yet
> England has charms to me, I have felt how sad
> It is to look across the dim cold sea
> That melancholy rolls its refluent stones
> Between us and the dear regretted land
> We call our own –

The poet-heroine asks what can the promise be for the stateless. She has a vision of France after the Reign of Terror, 'thick strewn/with various Death'. Famine, burning villages, plundered peasantry and incessant rain are devastating the land. A small episode of fear and outrage is drawn – a woman protects her child from the exploding shell. The poem ends with a prayer that 'These ill-starved wanderers' will regain their native country 'to fix/The Reign of Reason, Liberty and Peace'.

'Reason, Liberty and Peace' are not accidentally chosen as qualities to restore the broken nation. These are qualities of the Enlightenment and of the French Revolution itself, for Charlotte was no defender of reaction. Her love of liberty and her respect for French ideals is both intellectual, from her reading, and experiential, from her sojourn in that country. At one stage she left her husband in debtors' prison and took a rented house in Normandy. It was cheaper then to live in France than to survive in Sussex. (Where are our equivalent cheap escapes? Is it winter on the Costa Brava where it is cheaper than fuel bills with tax in England?) Like her novel's heroine, Emmeline, she was both shocked and intrigued by the social and economic differences between the two countries so geographically close to each other:

> But, however beautiful the outline, the landscape still appeared unfinished, dark and ruinous hovels, inhabited by peasants frequently suffering the extremes of poverty, half-cultivated fields, wanting the variegated enclosures that divide the lands in England; and trees often reduced to bare poles to supply the inhabitants with fuel, made her recollect with regret the more luxuriant and happy features of her native country.
>
> (*Emmeline*)

Emmeline dare not wander far from her temporary home because of the threatening aspect of the population. Even the women were 'robust and masculine'.

Charlotte, however, did wander far from her French home. Indeed she never seemed to stay for long anywhere after leaving comfortable, secure Bignor. We know that she visited Paris and saw scientific curiosities. We also know that she made friends with English visitors to pre-revolutionary France, for a few years later, in Brighton, she was visited by a young poet, an admirer who had bought her poems when he was a Cambridge undergraduate. In 1791 William Wordsworth, en route for that ever-memorable second journey for France, took a packet-boat from Brighton to France. Before he departed he visited the admired sonneteer and, it is said, received from her introductions to the Francophile, Helen Maria Williams and, even more politically, Brissot, the Girondin leader. Charlotte, still engaged in the fervour of liberty, was in the process of writing *Desmond*, her pro-revolutionary novel.

This was the author whose personal knowledge of suffering was matched by her vision of the pain of nations and of their oppressed peoples. Her pictures of the poor in France and of the battlefield in the American War of Independence are not unlike Wordsworth's memory in *The Prelude* of seeing the hungry, listless young girl with a wretched cow in a French lane, for her descriptions are graphic yet realistic. Suffering was her forte. Why did she suffer so?

The western edges of the Sussex plain, where, unlike at Brighton, the Downs withdraw from the sea and gently roll upwards into the broad hills, framing the Hampshire Basin, are the sites for small, comfortable market towns where, for brief intervals, Charlotte lived. I choose a window seat in the Army and Navy restaurant in Chichester. Here you can observe the life of the small cathedral city in West Street (there are also East, North and South but not many more streets). The passers-by are dwarfed by the north wall of the Cathedral protected by its attendant chain of tall, bare trees. Their serenity calms the hurried shoppers below. It is a wintry evening and the necklace of lights on the trees is a discrete, comfortable city gesture at Christmas decorations. I take Earl Grey and turn my attention along the street from my protected vantage: the road is lined with a variety of cars, expensive some of them, some of them not so new. All are packing in a precious freight of children from the school that discharges its red-blazered obligations in the safe havens of leather or plastic. It is a time of maternal protectiveness, the swooping-up of responsibilities, the daily ritual of responsibility for the seedcorn of the future. Are any like Charlotte, bravely fighting debt alone? Who are the single parents in the line of protectresses along West Street? Why did Julian die so young? Why must I carry on with private education? Am I being assertive or showing a lack of courage? Will it be worth it, all this expense while I work out next year's shoes and the mortgage and the costs of the years to come?

Charlotte's error was to marry a financial disaster – or perhaps it was her father's fault, marrying her to what must have looked like a safe catch, at a time when he was marrying again. One of her characters, Mrs Stafford, had the same fate:

> Mr Stafford was one of those unfortunate characters who, having neither perseverance and regularity to fit them for business, or taste and genius for more refined pursuits, seek in every casual occurrence of childish amusement, relief against the tedium of life. Tho' married very early, and tho' the father of a numerous family, he had thrown away the time and money, which should have provided for them in collecting baubles, which he had repeatedly possessed and discarded, 'till having exhausted every source that the species of idle folly offered, he had been driven by the same inability to pursue proper objects, into vices yet more fatal to the repose of this wife, and schemes yet more destructive to the fortunes of his family.
>
> (*Emmeline*)

It was not just a misjudged alliance, nor even just a bad marriage; it was a destructive disaster. Remember that until very recently a married woman's property, unless ingeniously protected by her former family, became the property of her husband. So it was in Charlotte's case. Eventually, after a series of bad debts and share crises, bankruptcy followed and, in the manner of the time, Benjamin Smith was put away into debtors' prison. His fate was his wife's fate. In 1784, Charlotte, then the mother of nine children (she was to have one more), lived with him in the confines of that grim jail. Far away now were the open Downs and the sweet pastures of the River Arun of her Sonnet, 'On leaving a part of Sussex':

> The Enthusiast of the Lyre who wander'd here,
> Seems yet to strike his visionary shell,
> Of power to call forth pity's tenderest tear,
> Or wake wild frenzy from her hideous cell!
> (*Elegiac Sonnets,* Sonnet XLV)

It was from the confines of the King's Bench Division that Charlotte issued forth in order to attempt to persuade a publisher to take her two books of sonnets for publication. Rejection was her everyday fare. She emerged from this dreadful time to survive by her own redoubled efforts of writing. She did more than survive – she did well by her children. Those that survived infancy were all educated. The boys had jobs found in India and in the early Civil Service. The girls were educated to be eligible. Charlotte's novels provided their food, their shelter and their education. Her ability at French assisted income. She translated *Manon Lescaut.* Who could criticize her for quoting French, when the occasion permitted it, in her novels? Maria Edgeworth could. She thought it vulgar. Vulgar or not, Charlotte was a survivor, but at a price.

Finally, the transect across Sussex must end at the sea. The fringe of alluvium provides the marshes and hard edges of the shore, but the sea sneaks up and destroys its own deposited memory and lays bare the ridged sands and transient clays that emerge the other side of the geological welkin in the terraces of the Thames around London. The Middleton beach is quiet and discreet, even on a warm Bank Holiday. Peaceful houses hide behind tamarisks or low hedges of privet which have shaken off the salt left by the last storm. No promenade here, just a broad stretch of grass with half a dozen small boats that never go out to sea, and tussocks of dry grass, tall yellow flowers and delicate pale stock that catch the winds. I listen for a long-lost sound, the bell of the old church, St Nicholas, of Middleton. The church began to lose its place on the clay bank, sapped by the angry, determined Channel, at the end of the eighteenth century. Constable sketched it before it finally disappeared. Rumours still circulate about boys playing football with skulls washed out of the engulfed churchyard. There Charlotte composed a sonnet on a suitably romantic topic, earthly destruction, the peace of death in balance against inner turmoil:

> With shells and sea-weed mingled, on the shore
> Lo! their bones whiten in the frequent wave;
> But vain to them the winds and waters rave;
> *They* hear the warring elements no more:
> While I am doom'd – by life's long storm opprest,
> To gaze with envy on their gloomy rest.
> (*Elegiac Sonnets*, Sonnet XLIV)

No passing bells here! No bones are washed up now, only an occasional remnant of metal, a wartime mine gone to sleep, a piece of upturned wreckage from the Channel's past. The sun shines on a new shore. At Elmer there is a new artificial cliff. Great boulders from Exmoor, two at a time on long lorries, have been brought to the shore and a massive curve of rocks built to protect the bungalows and holiday villas from the winter wave which 'o'er the shrinking land sublimely rides'.

Charlotte Smith's engraver would have appreciated the Elmer Rocks. An engraving opposite Sonnet XII ('Written on the sea shore – October 1784,' *Elegiac Sonnets*) shows a weeping woman perched below a great hard cliff face. A few

But the wild gloomy scene has charms for me,
And suits the mournful temper of my soul.

inches below her feet the sea froths and a boat is lifted out of the horizontal. There were no cliffs like that between the Isle of Wight and Brighton but, if her ghost wishes to pose in a simulation of despair, the erratic rocks of Elmer's coastal screen will do for a melancholy panorama.

The sea was invariably her place of deepest melancholy, in contrast to the Downs, which evoked memories of liberty and spirited joy. The wild, gloomy scene has charms 'and suits the mournful temper of my soul', but its attraction has darker moods. Like Cowper's castaway, engulfment in sorrow is close. Sonnet XLIII compares her fate to that of an exile on a bleak, foreign coast who momentarily may be tricked by a cloud's appearance as a sail, then sinks into deeper despair. In *Emmeline*, the hero, Godolphin, has a comfortable house near Cowes which is fortunate to be surrounded by woodland, protecting it from 'that look of bleakness and desolation which often renders a situation so near the sea unpleasant except in the months of summer'.

Her poem 'Elegy' (included in *Elegiac Sonnets*) inevitably involves the personal deluge, but equally inevitably the dying one takes with her the true cause of her sorrow, the gambler's sin:

> Loud and more loud, ye foaming billows, burst!
> Ye warring elements, more fiercely rave!
> Till the wide waves o'erwhelm the spot accurst
> Where ruthless Avarice finds a quiet grave!

A long way from Sussex, finally, for a last note on Charlotte Smith's sad memory, in another place in different domesticity, but in a prestigious company of sonnet makers. It is Christmas Eve 1802, in Dove Cottage, Town End Grasmere, also the eve of Dorothy Wordsworth's birthday:

> William is now sitting by me, at [1/2] past ten o'clock. I have been beside him ever since tea running the heel of a stocking, repeating some of his sonnets to him, listening to his own repeating, reading some of Milton's and the Allegro and Penseroso. It is a quiet, keen frost. Mary is in the parlour below attending to the baking of cakes, and Jenny Fletcher's pies. Sara is in bed in the toothache and so we are [alone]. My beloved William is turning over the leaves of Charlotte Smith's sonnets, but he keeps his hand to his poor chest, pushing aside his breastplate.

Readers have always assumed that the poet's pain was physical, but sympathy has its pressures too, felt deep in the heart.

A LITTLE LOCAL APOCALYPSE

Duncan Salkeld

And if you care to see the future look into the eyes of your young dancing children don't be afraid of our ways.

(Jefferson Airplane)

Not since 'the maniacs' left three cars burning on the apron had the old boys at the Military Aviation Museum at Tangmere been so incensed. Overnight, the disused airfield, which until 1970 served as 'home' to RAF Tangmere, had become an improvised 'park-up' for hundreds of New Age travellers on their way to celebrate the summer solstice at Stonehenge. The travellers had set out from a stretch of Sussex coastal towns: Brighton, Worthing, Arundel, Bognor Regis – children of the Weald and downland and sea shore – and gathered at Chanctonbury Ring before moving westward for their more sacred destination. The aviation chaps seethed when they imagined what effect this might have on summer visitors to the museum. But they needn't have worried. By 3.00 p.m. news went round that the travellers had all moved on, leaving behind only a few bags of rubbish and a huge sense of relief. The old boys had jeered as they left, waved two fingers and shouted what they all bloody well needed.

A convoy of battered vehicles snaked its passage through the ancient Sussex villages of Boxgrove, Lavant, Chilgrove and West Harting, and into the broad Hampshire countryside. The whole journey took three days, owing to the continual intervention of county police forces, who held up the convoy for vehicle and document checks every few miles. Eventually, the travellers arrived in Wiltshire, at the B312, which ran alongside fields of corn and broad beans not far from the immutable stones.

The sun gleamed on the windscreen of a yellow Dormobile as it came to a halt before a patrol car which blocked the road. Its

driver wound down the side window. He was in his early
twenties and, though he had left school without a single GCSE,
he had acquired a mildness and sense of responsibility that
neither housemasters nor parents had managed to instil in him
with their regimes. Christened William, his fellow travellers
knew him by the soubriquet 'Chy', which denoted his Cicestrian
place of conception. He would shyly explain sometimes that,
having grown up in a 'successful' family, he had joined the
travellers not so much out of modishness or principle as out of a
genuine need to escape the shouting and bullying of domestic
life. The travellers were a community which had welcomed him.
They didn't even query, let alone object to, his spending the night
under the stars. But most of all, they knew as he did what it was
to observe from a field the changing light of summer dusk on the
slopes of the Downs. At his 'naming' in the woods one night,
he'd been given the choice of 'Chy' or 'Young Boar', and the
latter he refused at the first opportunity. His partner, 'Tan', and
baby son, 'Biz-boz', were nicknamed the same night. Having
Tangmere parents, Emma's abbreviation was straightforward.
Biz-boz (Basil, after one of 'The Herbs') had been conceived one
warm evening beside the gentle flats at Bosham.

From the roadblock a policeman approached the van. Chy
leant out of the window. 'What is it, Officer?' he enquired. Tan
suckled the baby discreetly in the back of the van. Jefferson
Airplane played 'When the earth moves again' quietly on the
radio. The constable glanced twice at the mother and child and
then asked a question.

Dark, sheer, the stones grazed the light breeze with their
roughness. They stood in the night like giant shadows over
field mice that quivered and picked at the leavings of the
previous day. A mile away, fast asleep in his bed, Ted Bloat
turned over, taking the duvet with him. Molly, beside him,
snorted restlessly, pawed for the cover without success and
drifted back into silence. A distant thud had somehow
disturbed his repose. His mind settled once more around half-
remembered images. A holiday in the Witterings . . . Chichester
Cathedral . . . the spire down . . . its crumpled length lying

along the nave . . . its tip protruding into the Sailor's Chapel. . . .
He'd been aroused (something that only happened in his
dreams), but now that seemed to have subsided. He faded into
sleep, quite unaware that outside their window the world was
different. Huge black shapes hid low in the darkness like a
family of dead dinosaurs on the level of the Plain. Ten
thousand years of history were undone that night, and Ted
marked the occasion with a scratch.

The following morning at about six, the village began to
awake. The milkman had delivered, and the paper-boy and
postwoman were on their bikes. Ted got out of bed and made
for the curtains. The weather looked grey. They'd said it would
be sunny. No sign of the invaders. Yet.

'Why don't you and all your kind piss off back to where you
all came from?'

'We're visiting Stonehenge,' Chy offered doubtfully. 'What's
the problem?' Civilities were impossible: the word 'officer'
stuck in the craw.

'Well, apart from the fact that you are prohibited from
gaining access to the site, there's actually nothing there to see.'
The constable grinned. 'You see, it's gone. It all fell down last
night.' He stopped grinning. 'Right, turn your vehicle around
and leave the area immediately. If you don't, you and the
people in this vehicle will be arrested. Understand?' There the
conversation ended. No possibility of dialogue, of further
information or advice on routes: the uniform had spoken and
walked away. Chy swore at him uselessly.

'What is it?' called Tan from the back seat as she gently
winded Biz–boz after his feed.

Chy thought for a moment. 'Apparently it's not there. He says
it's fallen down,' he called back, blankly wondering at the sound
of his own words. He felt a little dazed. Then, dismissing the
whole idea as a stupid bourgeois-fascist joke, he put the
Dormobile into gear. 'We're going!' he shouted over his shoulder.

A dead sound came across the sky. It had happened before
but there was nothing to compare it to now. Huge and erect,
the broad stones of the Plain shouldered their massive burdens

effortlessly in what anciently had been a near-perfect circle. Then, in a second – a series of seconds – centuries of stillness suddenly edged into movement. Somewhere down in subterranean darkness, rock collapsed and the earth moved, extruding into lines of fissure and tiny channels. Water dispersed and clay sagged. One of the great Sarsen stones in the Outer Circle – quarried long ago from the Plain – felt the pressure of physical forces hitherto untried. The stones, whose gentle humming lulled the stars to sleep and kept their fierce lights at bay, ceased their astral song. They listened. Then came destruction all at once. No. 29 was the first of the monoliths to shift with the stress. It pitched 0.75 degrees south-east against its lintel, just sufficient to skew the horizontal stone asquint on its adjacent plinth, pushing that one forward while at the same time dragging the first with it, till the whole trilithon came crashing clumsily down. Things fell apart: the tenons and mortises could no longer hold. Driven by the lintel on top, stone 30 smashed into trilithon 1 and 2, jinking each column from its ancient wedge in the ground and ramming hard against No. 3, splaying the next trilithon, 4 and 5, and so on into 6 and 7. Chalk slumped and solifluction underground succeeded in bringing down stones elsewhere on the henge. The Inner Circle of Blue stones, so arduously cut from the hills of Prescelli, dressed and transported – who knows how? – to Wiltshire – that too collapsed as the ground cracked beneath it. Stone on stone, they seared, scarred and cracked one another as they fell. Tiny shards of silica and rhyolite splintered in the moonlight, and dust filled the black air. The stars burned fiercely and blinked.

Early that morning, Ted noticed a change in the prospect from their living room window. 'Molly!,' he called, 'Moll! Bloody 'ell. Come and see . . . it's gone. Come and look.' Molly finished in the kitchen and came through. Ted peered intently through the double glazing, at something she could not see. She strained over his shoulder, but he wouldn't move over for her to look, so instead she fumbled the seat of his trousers, warmly. Still he peered through the window: still she longed

A Little Local Apocalypse

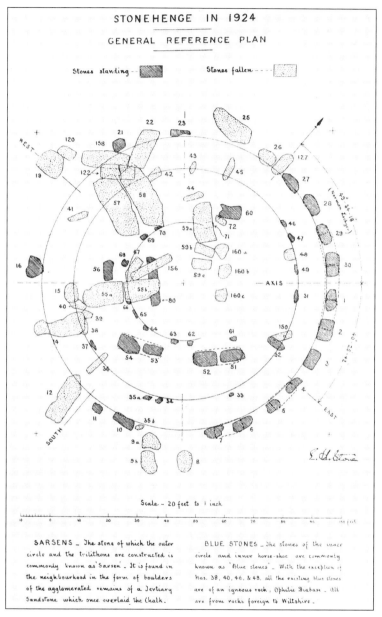

A plan of Stonehenge based on that of Professor Flinders Petrie, published 1880.

139

for some response. It was all so familiar. Thirty years of marriage could not disguise the fact that he had never really been interested in women, not in that way at least. Once more, she said nothing. 'Look!' said Ted, and he whistled with disbelief, still peering. Molly looked silently away.

Later that morning, the board of the recently privatized Stonehenge Foundation convened in haste and noise to consider urgent business in hand. There was much disorder. An inquiry must be set up, but its jurisdiction was complicated. Whitehall didn't seem to want to know, judging by the already numerous and futile phone calls, and disagreement was now palpable as to who should sit on the inquiry – palaeontologists, geologists, archaeologists, architects, historians? And which institutions should be involved – Devizes museum? The universities of Bath, Bristol, Oxford? Bath and Bristol were already shouting at each other over the table. Bristol's hypothesis was largely tectonic – a kind of mini earthquake; Bath had always been against the idea of building a motorway underneath the site and now just look at what had happened. Vera Binns of the Plain Lovers Campaign (PLC) wanted to know what was to be done.

'We'll just have to put them back up,' said one.

'They're not skittles or garden gnomes!' insisted another.

'Shouldn't we just let history take its course?' someone else complained.

'Here we raze our Ebenezer,' quipped the dry young clerk to the Bishop of Bath and Wells. There was quiet. Everyone glared at him. 'Sorry,' he muttered hopefully. Then tumult began again. The loss to tourism was incalculable.

But not for Ted who, at his curtains, was already making plans to collect pieces of ancient Britain for informal sale to interested collectors.

The police had not been entirely successful in stemming the flow of travellers seeking a way through to the site where they could celebrate the summer solstice. Rumours had gone round about the roadblocks and diversions, and about the stones, which made the travellers all the more determined to achieve their goal. The only solution was to abandon vehicles, brightly painted affairs with John Lennon headlamps, and make route by espadrille or bare feet to the henge to do there simply whatever they could. No one quite knew what. A police helicopter buzzed overhead as a crowd of travellers sifted into lines and tramped row by row through the beanfield. A ragged army of the faithful, some with a philosophy, others with dogs, collected at the main road. There were half-naked Jesuses with catkin hair, dungareed Magdalenes all bangles and abacus beads, and a handful of bewildered small children. They belonged to diverse groups or none at all – among them mystics, visionaries, musicians, dancers, jugglers, anarchists and, maybe, the ecological poetry collective. An improvised gathering of small tribes – sons of God and the daughters of men – together they crossed the A303 and came against the perimeter fence that separated them from the stones. Shocked at the sight of the megaliths scythed to the ground, they pulled down the wire and rushed onto the Plain, Chy in their midst clasping Tan's hand, and Biz-boz – swaddled Third World style around her shoulders – beginning to cry. The police had regrouped on foot and now formed a menacing rank of dark blue in front of the stones. They wore riot gear. The travellers advanced, fearful and angry.

The buttons on Commander Stukeley's tunic shone in the sun. He rocked on his heels, hands behind his back, and surveyed the field. Hannibal, Alexander, Schwartzcopf, Stukeley. He seemed pleased. He spoke into a small radio. At a signal, the dark blue line broke up and charged towards the nearing crowd. Travellers ran everywhere. There were screams, shouts and the whizz of bottles, stones, anything, flying through the air and raining down on the police. Things quickly got out of hand. Scuffles started and then real fighting broke out. People were snatched by the hair and dragged screaming to one side. Others, women among them, were shoved to the ground and beaten. Two were arrested on suspicion of being former IRA terrorists. In the pitched battle, Chy suddenly found himself separated from Tan and he couldn't see where

she was. He looked round anxiously. Batons were out and
someone went down hard on the ground beside him. It wasn't
Tan, thank God. A policeman stumbled past bleeding from the
ear. Chy struggled through the crush of bodies, clawing and
ducking his way out to open ground. Still he could not see Tan
and Biz-boz. Then he found himself beside the stones. Turning
about, he saw close-up the catastrophe of their demise.
Something made him sob as he viewed each rock fallen. He
clambered up on No. 80 and with his hand smoothed its hard,
cold grain, as if to succour it, somehow to ease its silent dying.
The stone was cold. Then, standing up, he looked once more
for Tan and Biz-boz. From the periphery of the field, his
upraised form appeared as vaunting exultation to the unlucky
vision of Commander Stukeley's burning eye. Catching sight of
him there – unbeliever in the temple, heathen on the stones
with muddy boots, violator . . . accursed! – something clicked
and whirred in the Commander's brain like a mad insect
buzzing franticly. Straining at the fray, then at the blasphemer
on the stones, it saw blood.

The Commander started away from his colleagues by the
entrance gate and ran screaming onto the Plain. He was jabbering,
flailing his arms in the air, and shouting and crying all at once. He
rushed, unnoticed at first, into the throng in the direction of the
stones. He kicked with his black boots and smashed with his
baton. Still he screamed and wept, thrashed and howled. Chy
looked up, hearing some sort of falsetto amid the crowd. He
caught the blurred image of a figure in black stumbling its way out
of the mêlée. At first the figure's words were dull and unclear.
Then, as it came closer, Chy began to make them out. Tears
poured down the Commander's face as he ejaculated to the skies:

> Magnificent love . . . and above were costly stones . . .
> Heavenhell in subterranean grounds of deepfession . . . after the
> measure of hewed stones . . . through lightning, thunder, hail,
> current thunderstorms . . .. He was a widow's son . . . came
> Hiram Ahtrobant Light who hearing . . . and his father was a
> man of Tyre . . . syllables unfruitfulness . . . cunning to work all

works in brass . . . in the plague nice taste love can things . . . he was filled with wisdom . . . eicksstract mopfjum opfjum goulard justiformpowder . . .. Behold the heaven and heaven of heavens cannot contain thee. . . . Oh how many more things I have. . . .

Chy wiped the blur from his eyes. 'Dad!' he shouted, 'Dad!' The Commander's eyes rolled vacantly. 'Dad!' Chy shouted again, pleading for recognition.

The Commander stopped at the stone's side, groaned and swayed. The whirr and buzz in his brain was unremitting. Chy looked confusedly round for Tan and Biz-boz, but they were nowhere to be seen. He hoped they were safe and began to clamber down. As he did so, the Commander lurched forward, reached out blindly over the stone and gripped Chy tight by the throat. 'Dad!' his son gasped. 'Dad!' Chy choked out the word as distinctly as he could. The pressure of the man's fingertips felt like a spike in his neck. 'Da'!' Air seemed to escape Chy's lungs without sound. His face reddened, then darkened, and his eyes widened. The Commander gazed peculiarly at the hordes around him. The Lord provided no ram from the thicket so he pressed again, harder this time. Gradually, he felt the thing weaken and its weight go limp. The insect buzzed wildly in his head and gradually died down. Anguished and exhausted, he let go and sat on the grass beside the stone. The Temple lay in ruins, Gog and Magog were fallen but their enemies were defeated. He remained on the ground insensible. Faintly, at last, between gasps for air, he began to murmur:

> There is a Hand to turn the time,
> Though thy Glass today be run,
> Till the Light hath brought the towers low
> Find the last poor Trav'ler one . . .
> And a Soul in ev'ry stone.

The stars burned a little less fiercely. The old boys could laugh at it now, as they took their hats and coats, locked up and bade each other goodnight.

. . . AND A WHIFF OF FISH PASTE

Margaret Nakra

> The traditional understanding of change assumes and requires
> not only the independence of entities from our representations
> of them, but the independence of our representations from the
> criteria by which they are judged; but if those criteria, those
> measures of adequacy and accuracy, are no less community – or
> paradigm – specific than the facts they are intended to measure,
> confirmation or validation would seem to be at once assured
> and empty; and since the procedures of validation, the
> description to be validated, and the object in relation to which
> validity is to be assessed are homologous, the analyst who uses
> the perspective of any one to get a purchase on the others is
> apparently engaged in a circular and futile exercise.
>
> (Stanley Fish)

My young nephew had come to stay. It was all an adventure: a
first trip to England; travelling alone; exchanging the heat of
Delhi's summer for Chichester's late spring – even the deal that
he should speak only English became part of a game. You need
to know all this for this story to work.

Returning home to Chichester after a trip to the beach, my
friend Annie was behaving like some demented tourist guide.
She pointed out the Downs and the windmills; became excited
when she spotted the sign to the 'butterflies and gardens' at
Earnley – not that she had ever been there, 'but the children
would enjoy it' – and finished the whole thing off by informing
anyone who was listening that the cathedral spire that we
could see dominating the skyline was the only spire that could
be seen from the sea. We all agreed that it is an impressive sight
– and it is. No matter how many times I might see it, there is,
paradoxically, a visceral pleasure as the spire comes into view.
And the cynic – one of the roles that I am adopting in this story
– might point out that, although it makes for very dangerous

driving, to keep one's eyes turned heavenwards as one approaches the 'historic city' that I call home has one big advantage: one can overlook, literally, the transport depots, motels and supermarkets (one once a burned-out shell, but that's another story) that encircle the city.

'What did Annie mean when she said that the cathedral was posing?' Ashok asked with a worried look. I couldn't think what he meant, and I will cut the account of the following twenty minutes or so as we recreated Annie's commentary of the previous evening. We finally decided that she had said that the cathedral is imposing – but I prefer Shoky's version: the cathedral does pose; indeed, the whole of the inner city poses. Much is made of the buildings that remain from the seventeenth and eighteenth centuries, and, like a coquette of that period, the city sticks its patches to its face and sets out to seduce. It generally succeeds. It helps, of course, if that particular charm appeals – if it does, then a walk through the Pallants, particularly North Pallant with its fine Georgian architecture, finds Chichester at its most seductive. And even if one is immune to that surface charm, it would require a very determined frigidity not to thaw as the late evening sunshine catches the red-tiled roofs and chimney-pots of the cottages that hug the outer side of the city walls. This is one of the great pleasures of the city: one can walk around it with ease. There are few cars to compete with; parks and gardens link various roads; coffee-houses abound (actually, so do pubs, but coffee-houses seem more appropriate to the mood).

There is, however, a strange ritual that local ladies engage in when walking around the streets that branch out from the Market Cross. These are the ladies that in another story keep lace-edged handkerchiefs in drawers scented with lavender. It's these same handkerchiefs that are an integral part of the ritual, particularly on Wednesdays, which is Market Day. For towards the bottom of East Street, not very far from the site of the market, is Shippam's, suppliers of fish paste to the Queen. (Yes, really, the Royal Arms above the main entrance confirms that the Queen has, or has had, sardine paste for tea, just like you

*East Pallant and
(below) West Pallant,
Chichester.*

or me.) Of all the buildings in Chichester, it was Shippam's that gave me the most pleasure when I first settled in the city. D.H. Lawrence writes of the influence of hymns in a man's life: for a child of the fifties the influence is more likely to be the early television advertisements; and for me, who endured/experienced/enjoyed a nonconformist upbringing, choruses and advertisements got curiously jumbled, so that I couldn't work out if I was shining in my small corner at the bidding of Jesus or a toothpaste manufacturer. But back to Shippam's. Can you remember the silly song that accompanied its early advertisements that went something like 'Shippam's for tea, for tea, for tea . . .' and was sung to the tune of the Blue Danube waltz? I can't remember what came next, but the ads obviously worked. After Sunday school, my grandmother would give me 'a little treat' – fish paste on toast followed by jelly and condensed milk. For me, fish paste became inextricably associated with Sundays and love. So I moved to the city where such childhood delights are manufactured (alright, I exaggerate, but . . .). But why didn't I ever wonder how those fish got minced up and packed into those little glass jars? A recent browse through some of the Shippam's archive (kept at the splendid local museum) provides the source for so many stories. There is a photograph of three trestle-tables on which large joints of meat and plucked fowl are neatly arranged – the fowl lying on their backs, their necks artistically bent over the edge of the table. Alongside the tables are racks of fish, unskinned. You are now free to complete this little bit of the tale – I have become an uncompromising vegetarian, so my account would be biased! The advertising archive is fascinating: I had always thought that Shippam's made 'meat and fish paste', but by 1962 one could be ordering chicken breasts in jelly, calves' tongues, and liver and bacon paste. One was encouraged to try 'bloater paste on hot toast', but I cannot remember Gran doing so; certainly she didn't try 'anchovy paste for cocktail parties'.

I know, you are wondering where the ladies and their hankies have gone. There is a postscript to the Shippam's tale. I was told

View (looking out) from North Walls, Chichester.

a story about a photograph of Shippam's factory and its surroundings. By the time the photograph was used in publicity displays a prominent chimney had 'disappeared' from it. (Do check out this story in the local museum where the evidence is held.) Oh yes, handkerchiefs *are* needed, or perhaps it should be nosegays if we are keeping with the 'historical city' story.

This piece is not being written at one sitting. This morning I am sitting at my desk overlooking my walled garden and the roofs of the houses in my street. It has been raining, and everything has a hosed-down look. I do not want to continue yesterday's story: I had intended to point out how many tourist attractions have saints' names – St Mary's Hospital, now an almshouse, in St Martin's Square; the former church of St Peter

*Chichester
Cathedral from
Canon Lane.*

the Great, now a shopping arcade; and the now redundant church of St John the Evangelist, built in 1612. Whatever guide to Chichester one picks up, these saints are listed – how strange then that St Joseph is overlooked. St Joe's, as it is affectionately called, attracts its share of visitors to Chichester. Offering a bed, and more besides, St Joe's is the local night refuge. Founded, in part, by those who were appalled that in this 'glorious city' a man who had been sleeping rough could die in a public lavatory, St Joe is the unacknowledged saint in the city's publicity material.

'How unpleasant it is to be locked out', Woolf wrote, and then added, 'how it is worse perhaps to be locked in'. Thank goodness for my fluorescent gnome! I live 'within the walls' and heed Woolf's words when I fear that I am perpetuating the grand narrative of Chichester: avoiding pvc windows; creating a garden appropriate to our old house. Of course, numerous households behaving in this way make the city beautiful; but our gnome seems to keep the worst excesses of city-pickling at bay – it is our household's act of defiance. And we are not alone – all over the city there is evidence of little acts of defiance. One of the nice things about Chichester is that it allows busking, though not without a fight. So one can wander the streets to the sound of Vivaldi or gentle folk tunes. (I have just been reminded that there is an Elvis impersonator; but this is my version.) There is a couple who are heavily into folk music: he dresses in denim and plays a banjo, she has a long wrap-around skirt and sings – but at the final chorus she unwraps her skirt, revealing purple sequinned hotpants and silver cuban-heeled shoes, and tap dances across the pedestrian precinct to the increasingly fast music. It only works once, but it's wonderful. Less dramatic are the misericords, those hidden fantasies of bored choristers, in the cathedral; the bespectacled face peering down from the cathedral wall onto Paradise whose incongruity pleases; the saucy lady on the wall of the local wine bar who is fighting the planning officer at this very moment for the right to wink. The golden fish that managed a short time on the roof of the local fish restaurant lost its fight, but the leaping dolphin in St Martin's Street remains – perhaps because it is the work of John Skelton.

Three or four years ago I was told of a gardener on a local estate who created a garden fitting for a country house; but behind a high wall was his own garden where he grew speedwells instead of grass and produced a blue lawn (the story of the blue lawn at West Dean is oft repeated in Chichester). But it was a private garden, and the man moved and I never had the opportunity to see this blue lawn, but it lay alongside my gnome in my mind. Then recently I saw that this man was creating a 'surreal' garden in the old walled gardens at Stansted House just a few miles west of Chichester.

'The entrance fee is £1.01 – a pound for the garden and a penny for the art – or a lobster or seven shells or a prism', I was informed when I phoned for information. Not being Gerard de Nerval, I took my purse! At the entrance to the garden, visitors are invited to enter 'with an open mind' – oh, I did, I did – but 'open' does not mean blank, and I entered with expectations and experience. The expectations were, in part, raised by the publicity surrounding the creation of the garden (a TV programme; articles in glossy magazines; entries in local travel guides) and by the explanation offered by the designer that 'the overall design is loosely based on the concept of the "world-tree" . . . the cosmic tree represents the universe with the roots in the underworld, the trunk as the real world and the branches as Heaven. . . .' So I entered. Have you ever tried to 'read' a garden? Among the profusion of plants, artefacts are placed/discarded/thrown around. Mirrors, ladders, rusting metal objects, buckets of dung, broken terracotta pots – do they mean anything or is it some private joke? Much of the symbolism is rather obvious – the pagoda-like structure, made out of what looks like cable drums, invites thoughts on the seven cosmic stages; ladders can be seen as symbols of access to the sacred or, following Freud, as a disguised expression of sexual desire. The obvious linking of shells (many of which are scattered around the garden) to the female genitalia is disconcerting when the number of severed, female forms that encircle a stagnant pool is noted. There is something unsettling about this garden. It's not the fact that a plastic lobster rests on a lawnmower (I'm reminded of Dali's *Lobster Telephone*) or that a garden roller is rendered unusable for its conventional purposes by the addition of metal scrolls (echoes of Duchamp?); no, these are obviously 'unsettling' ploys.

What I find considerably more questionable are the tortured forms of young saplings; plants twisted and pinned in unnatural shapes; spread-eagled trees reminding me, in the context of the heavy sexual imagery, of gynaecological examinations – and I was making this visit primarily as an avid gardener!

So I went back to the entrance and started again. Next to a deep purple buddleia the most beautiful butterfly had settled on a painted drainpipe; giant thistles rose high above exuberant planting. It was a warm, still day and any noise seemed part of the design of the garden: what wind there was rustled the surrounding pines, and the crunching sound made by feet on shingle ceased when we stepped off the path to wander over grass mown into circles. I coveted plants I could not name and was cheered by evidence of mildew. And then the most extraordinary thing happened: a peahen strutted down the path and settled herself in front of a mirror: talk about the suggestiveness of accidental images; Breton must have had something similar in mind. Yet even this delight did not erase the unease I felt in this garden; perhaps things are too random, too rusty, too racked.

I bought some plants and left.

Coda: a number of years ago the gardener at West Dean was asked how to remove speedwells from a lawn. He replied that he would cultivate the speedwells and rake out the grass. Of such incidents are tales created – there was no blue lawn behind a high wall; but then, few have seen my fluorescent gnome.

Bird swallowing a fish: Henri Gaudier-Brzeska.

THREE POEMS

Rob Batho

Bignor Hill

South, below Bignor Hill,
Just above Gumber Bothy,
We stop on the flinty track
And look over downland
To Slindon, Middleton and the sea.

Our conversation putters to a stop.
The breeze sinks.
The warm air-waves hover
Jazzled by bird call.
And there, over the hawthorn hedge
In a field of sage green wheat
A chaffinch is perched impossibly
On a single head of corn.

Stubbs Wood

Even in the hottest and driest of summers
When dust powders hedgerows,
Grasses flop and fade
And the earth cracks like crockery,
You can follow a chalky downland trail
As it curls out of the midday sun
Into the dense dusk of a beechwood
And find, settled in the ruts of tractor tracks,
Two pools as cool as snow
And darker than winter.

Bognor Seafront

Old beach huts doze
and pebbles slope away
through wooden groynes
to the flat sands and mirrored pools.

From the pale lapping shallows
an arc of black rocks
step out
and stutter
to a halt
beyond the legs of the pier.

A dark arm of land
curls in from the west.

The sky as wide as a deep breath
And the sea stretches to meet it.

Bognor Rocks – with seabirds.

FROM RACTON TOWER TO THE POETRY OF LIGHT

Paul Foster

This is a journey of darkness and light;
A journey of joyous gloom and the fortune
Of folly and temptation. It will begin
In Sussex and end in Sussex, but before
The final word there will be a great
Searching that 'about . . . and about must go'
Even to the high mountains. On the way
We will meet fools and virgins, poets and painters,
Kings and Jews, and will be accompanied
By a constant companion, friend I might
Think, who will say little but provoke
Much – which is the best way for friends
To contribute for, as Auden said,
Truth is a reticence, and one must learn
How not to say more than is needed.

It was late October and the weather, quiet and still, was perfect
for a journey. But which journey? That was the puzzle. If it was
to be above ground, it was an ideal opportunity for Racton, to
renew acquaintance with its prophetic monument to an imperial
dream. But it was also just the right weather for a quite
different journey, for a journey best described as below ground
– for when the weather is set for digging, it is better to get on
with the task. Racton, I decided, would have to wait – and so,
seizing a rake, spade and bucket, I set off down the garden.
Clusters of berries on the holly arch were already tinged red,
and the ivy, trailing over the smooth grey bark, was bursting for
bloom. I ducked under some hanging branches and sensed a
sticky pull: a fine cicatrice of web had caught my cheek and, as
I rubbed, an orb spider deftly dropped, and safe against the

blunder of a biped, disappeared into a crack between the stones of the path. I turned and moved on to the vegetable patch: it was the soil and its hidden solemnities that beckoned.

There's something substantial, faintly regal even, about potatoes. The growers know it too when they name varieties: Majestic, British Queen, King Edward, Ulster Sceptre, Red King, Duke of York – although there may be more of mischief than favour in some of the decisions. And yet, the way a single tuber, no larger than the egg of a cackling hen, can turn in the space of six months' darkness underground into a bucket of beauties the size of goose eggs is more than any monarch can achieve. And as I gathered the piles of dried haulm into heaps for burning, a fitting irony, at least in this part of Sussex, struck me forcibly. Was it not on the shores of a local village (Bosham) that the dark silence of a sea tide had mocked the majesty of one such monarch, Canute, and driven him from the beach like a scrap of flotsam caught in a sea breeze? But potatoes, however one might rue their names, are different. The visible work of their vast stems is to leaf, flower, droop and, yellow with age, spotted with disease, wither and fall; but during this cycle, below ground there occur invisible events that must have amazed, even crazed, the early planters. Perhaps – I bent to break off a handful of dried grass and add it to a pile of oak leaves to make a base to burn the haulm – there was a whole social history connected to the potato. When the visible and the invisible are so strikingly in contention . . . but it was heat I needed, so I struck a match and dabbed it into the grass. The flame ran along the stalks, the leaves crackled and into the still air a steady column of pale smoke rose above the garden to fade into the mist above, as thin as skimmed milk.

With the haulm burning, I set to work with relish. There is a season for everything, and compost, seven or eight barrow-loads of rotted and crumbly richness from under the large laurel on the lawn, would not be trenched in until next spring. So the job was rough digging and collecting the tubers that had been missed when the different varieties had been lifted earlier. The first earlies had been finished in July (I grow only two rows and they are dug very carefully), but the four rows of second earlies and six rows of maincrop, now safely in store, usually meant a half-bucket of leavings: dug and cooked fresh from the garden they provided a satisfying meal before the glooms of winter.

Spade in, push down, lift and turn; spade in, push down, lift and turn. The ground was very shallow in this part of the garden, not much more than a spit deep above the flint and chalk, which was why in the spring I would trench and set the chitted seed in compost. The accumulated rhythm of work soon warmed muscle and blood, and as I progressed – push, lift, turn – there came to my mind a few words. At first they were easily ignored, but with every lift and turn the freshly exposed earth before me spread ever wider and finally I paused to listen:

> Racton Tower is . . .
>
> Racton Tower is fall . . .
>
> Racton Tower is falling down,
>
> > falling down, falling down. Hey!
>
> Racton Tower is falling down, falling down –
>
> Hey! mort stone;
>
> Hey! mort stone.

That was it! Such a catchy thing, even jolly; and (as I glimpsed an earthworm wriggling back into the wall of the spit) rather like a nursery rhyme, for the sense and the sound were at variance. The rhythm recalled youthful spring outings, carefree and eager, but the words were different: they dealt in final things – of mutability, decay, death. The contrast made me restless and, straightening the spade, I seized the bucket, already half-full, and made for the clematis bower and its sheltered seat.

Mounted on a low wall, with the trellis above, the whole bower was several decades old and the stiff stems, arching

*The decaying remains of
Racton Tower.*

towards the light like a woven awning, provided shelter in any
but the severest weather. The original planting, a scented white
Montana, was interlaced in spring with a cloudless blue
Alpina, but now there was only the last flowering of a
Tangutica to catch on its leathery yellow sepals the gleam of
the morning sun. The noise of the street was absorbed by the
thickly tangled stems and the quiet lent texture to my recall.

I had been to Racton and its tower on several occasions, but
a special resonance was attached to one occasion when the
cloud was low, the air still and damp, and the last leaves hung
limp at the end of oak and ash. Racton itself, a hamlet with a
church, farm and a few cottages, is scarcely six miles north-
west of Chichester – with open sea at East Head (West
Wittering), almost the same distance due south. Beyond,
travelling west, is Stansted, the last great house in Sussex, and
the county boundary with Hampshire. For three hundred
years, from Agincourt to a decade after the South Sea Bubble,
Racton had been home to a family called Gunter. A Colonel
George Gunter was recorded as performing notable service to

—*The Pharos at Stansted in Sussex 1771* —

A contemporary (Romantick) drawing of Racton – suggesting use as a lighthouse.

royalty. The future Charles II, in flight from the Battle of Worcester (1651), arrived in the south with no prepared transport across the Channel, and it was owing to Gunter's loyalty and resolve that passage was procured and that Charles sailed through Shoreham on 14 October. Whether the king passed through Racton is debatable, but adjacent to the church of St Peter, upright in its monuments to the Gunters, is a thatched and timber-framed dwelling recently painted in cream. It bears the name, King Charles' Cottage.

Whatever the truth of the association, if Charles had been at Racton on a day similar to the one I recount, it can be no surprise that he was attracted by the glitter of Paris. As I trudged along the lane, puddle after puddle of stale dankness offered neither reflection nor ripple, and across the fields and behind the hedges an oppressive silence filled the air.

I tried to keep my spirits up, and thought of what I might do if Dame Fortune led me to Paris, but the dream refused to form. And in any case, flesh and bone would be too weary even to contemplate that edifice of iron called the Eiffel Tower; the climb to Racton was sufficient for me.

The lane, marked by ancient hedgerows of oak and ash, hazel and hawthorn, wound up the slope of the down to a clump of deciduous trees. From afar, with the top of the tower above the skyline, it is easy to fear that some malign purpose is prepared – an industrial chimney threatening the countryside with the stench and grease derived from processing thousands of downland sheep, or perhaps the visible height of a breathing shaft for a world below, hungry for the moist air of rejuvenation. There must be enough creatures in the chalk to make the Downs dance, for as the poet says: 'In the bones of the rock/The fossils are living . . . moving,/Coiling, crawling,/ Aching for the sea.'

But close to, with the structure before me, malign speculation was replaced by a curious dislocation. To be effective, Gothick buildings are best observed in surroundings of grandeur (evocative of nature's terror and power) or as the backcloth to the mysterious, horrific in disbelief; and Racton offers neither. Despite the scale of intention – a triangular base of about forty-five feet on each side, with round towers at the corners, a stouter tower in the middle and each topped by another (smaller) tower – the present structure conveys a forlorn sadness. Great falls of flint cladding expose patches of bare brick; windows and huge doorways, bereft of sills, jambs and heads, gape demeaned; and within, heaps of rubble and refuse squat evilly, in a cavernous emptiness. Decaying grass, nettle and bramble abut the footings; and above, except for a perched outline hinting at an owl, *Athene noctua* (that hunter of voles and mice), no bird glides or sings.

Yet, beheaded as the towers are (the upper, smaller towers no longer stand), the fourfold trunk remains – upright too. If the architect, Theodosius Keene (*fl.* 1770–87), and his patron, George Montagu Dunk, second Earl of Halifax, were to see their creation today, empty and gloomy though it is, they could reflect that their work at Racton still beckons to succeeding ages. Further, they would see that the visitor of the 1990s can stand on the southern step of the glory that once was Racton Towers and glimpse, not what the 'traveller from an antique land' saw – 'bare . . . and level sands' – but a wide and rich expanse of coastal plain with, in the distance beyond, a shimmer and glint of water.

It was success across this water – Chichester Harbour, the English Channel and then the vast billows of the Atlantic – that led Halifax, President of the Board of Trade in the mid-eighteenth century, to be dubbed 'Father of the Colonies'. To this day the principal settlement of Nova Scotia bears his name and honours his prescience.

But if water helped Halifax to success, it was no good for me. It was fire I needed (left in cold water, potatoes just rot), so I got up from the seat and made for the kitchen. Preparation of food is one of the arts of life, in which the simple is as engaging as the sophisticated. A complex sauce, prepared through hours on the stove to the essence of its ingredients, may offer an experience as intense as the mathematical elegancies of a Bach fugue compressed to the sound of a single lingering call echoing through the galleried hall of a marbled mansion; but the homely – a platter of bread and cheese, brightly arranged with strips of pepper (green, red, yellow), slices of tomato and cucumber, apple or courgette – can satisfy a different kind of human necessity. When our head walks in the clouds, it is good to wrestle with the fruits of the earth.

Putting the bucket of leavings in the sink, I filled a saucepan with water and set it on the heat. Then, taking a brush, I cleaned the potatoes, cut out some slug damage with a Kitchen Devil and slid them into the pan. A scoop of salt, the lid aslant, adjust the gas – and there was twenty minutes, perhaps less, to pick a leaf or two of mint, some thyme (the dark purple and lemon), and a handful of late chives – and to see what I could discover about the history of potatoes. Miller must say something, and White, I recalled, wrote about growing them in the 1750s at Selborne in Hampshire.

Philip Miller, styled by his contemporaries as 'the Prince of Horticulture', was gardener at the Chelsea Physic Garden (the botanic garden of the Company of Apothecaries) from 1722 to 1770. But digging and planting, grafting and pruning, even with the necessary sowing, hoeing and harvesting, were insufficient for his energies, and in his spare time he prepared a dictionary of gardening practice that served the needs of horticulture for three generations. In a somewhat battered copy of the eighth and last edition of this work (1768), I read: 'The [Potato] was but little cultivated in England till of late.' For those of us brought up on the story of Raleigh's pleasure in the potato, such parsimony of planting seemed distinctly odd, but when I turned to the author of Selborne, Miller's account was confirmed. In a letter to Daines Barrington of 1778, White wrote: 'Potatoes have prevailed in this district . . . within these twenty years only.' He went on to explain that the reluctance shown by villagers had been overcome only by his own willingness to reward them for their labours 'with premiums'.

That the advantage of growing such a nutritious and reliable staple was won in the face of opposition of the severest kind is a credit to the quiet persistence and persuasion of good sense. But neither Miller nor White offers any explanation for what they describe, so – on a venture – I sought out a biography of White, and found an answer. There, in a note to an account of White's own practice in the growing of potatoes, I read this:

Although west of the Severn and north of the Trent potatoes flourished in the late seventeenth century, in south-east England it was not until the mid-eighteenth century that much progress was made, potatoes until that time being associated with leprosy, venery and other ills.

And further, in relation to Sussex, the author went on to claim that, in the 1760s, potatoes 'shared with Popery the indignation of the people and "No Popery, no potatoes!" was a popular cry at elections'.

So that was it! The dark workings of nature, multiplying invisibly underground a single tuber into a root fit for harvest, were identified with ill-health, with lust, with anything that was inexplicable.

'Keep still!' I muttered, as the potatoes (all eyes and toes) glinted and rolled in the frothy water, eluding my prodding fork. In another three minutes they would be ready, but still firm enough to cut and eat without collapsing into shapeless mash. To be satisfying, food needs to be resistant and, in flavour and texture, occasionally unpredictable; and especially so for vegetarians. What carnivores eat is recognizably (for those with even the briefest experience of the dissection bench and the butcher's shop) a matter of 'like eating like'; but for those who prefer static food – leaves, stems, fruit and earthy produce from below ground – there is always a delight in another world, resistant in its difference. And yet, paradoxically, that difference 'below ground' is best seen in higher ground, in the clear light of mountains, for it is in rarefied air that a greater resistance can be clarified – exposing weakness, gathering and revealing strength.

Then, quite sharply and suddenly as I idly tapped the fork on the side of the saucepan, there formed – through the rising steam and bubbling water – an angry landscape, cut with chasms and ravines, mountainous in rocks and cliffs. Deep in a darkening valley, cypress trees pointed upwards, and across a tall bluing sky, fists and knots of sandstone cloud heaved and hurt. Dominating the scene were two male figures. Robed in loose togas, the one, with an outstretched arm, gestured imperially; the other, seized by fear and a chilling hate, stumbled away on bare feet, his heavy wings of revolt and shame shuttered and clenched.

Not being accustomed to hallucinations (or visions), I gripped the handle of the saucepan. Strangers foretold in the flickering flames of a firegrate or in the dregs from a cup of China tea were one thing, but potatoes that could raise a landscape reminiscent of Aramaic Palestine were a different matter and required stern action. I swung round to the sink and, as I did, caught a flask of oil ('Extra virgin oil', the label read, 'Freshly pressed'). With a thud, the flask fell horizontal and rolled across the work surface, gushing oil in pale tongues of golden light. On the instant, the landscape dissolved and there burst from my lips:

> Paulsgrove! Paulsgrove!
> Light the Lamp
> At Paulsgrove!

But that was impossible (Paulsgrove is in the next county); and in any case, the potatoes needed to be drained for it was time for lunch, oil or no oil.

Perhaps it was this thought, of fullness and emptiness, or perhaps the oddity of filling a lamp with virgin oil, or some other (unrecognized) visual or verbal association, but as I settled to eat – potatoes, a dash of oil (from what was left in the flask), freshly ground black pepper, a sprinkling of sliced leaves of mint and lemon balm – I recalled that beyond the River Ems, the western boundary of Sussex with Hampshire, there ran from Havant to Fareham a ridge of chalk, culminating in Portsdown Hill.

From the highest point of this ridge, at about four hundred feet, one can survey the wide panorama of Langstone in the east; Spithead and the Isle of Wight in the south (where, on a clear day, the steeple of All Saints, Ryde, thrusts skyward); and in the west, Gosport peninsula with Lee Tower (built in 1935) poking up from the site of the former railway station and pier entrance. Dominating the view is Portsmouth, and the harbour that for so many centuries was at the centre of Britain's naval endeavour. So vital was this endeavour to the country's survival that just over a hundred years ago the fortifications at Portsmouth were the sternest in the world. Developed from a plan advocated by Lord Palmerston, new structures were added to existing defences so as to form a ring of protective forts. At the time when the plan was conceived there was a great fear of attack from across the Channel. The new forts, together with historic structures (Southsea Castle and Henry VIII's other castles in the area: Calshot, Hurst, Netley, Yarmouth and Cowes, all of which formed part of the earlier defences against invasion), were designed to make the harbour and its associated dockyard impregnable from the sea and, in the event of an encircling coastal invasion, from the land also.

Evidence of these structures is still startlingly present. To the west lie the remnants of the extensive works of Gosport: ramparts and gateways, moats and forts (Gomer, Grange, Rowner, Brockhurst, Elson, Monckton and Blockhouse, echoing still with the resonance of gunfire); to the south, in the midst of the Solent waters, crouch the great bastions of Horse Sand, Spit Bank, No Man's Land and St Helen's; and to the east is Cumberland Fort, built in 1746.

However, from Portsdown Hill the eye is caught by a far older structure: Portchester Castle. Washed by water on three sides, the outer walls, which enclose nine acres of ground, are Roman, as are fourteen of an original twenty bastions. The great keep and inner bailey, bound by a moat, are twelfth century, and so is the church – an outstanding Romanesque structure with many of its original features still intact. At the core of the defences are remains of a fourteenth-century palace built by Richard II. Such a complex of buildings from varying periods is in stark contrast to the uniformity of modern developments, one of which almost overlooks the castle. Stand on the shingle at the foot of the castle's outer walls and look to the north. Street after street of planned housing rise from the foreshore and in a symmetrical patterning ascend the southern slope of Portsdown, for this is Paulsgrove, an estate designed to meet Portsmouth's urgent need for housing following the Second World War.

From Portchester Castle, many of the details of the estate are indistinct, but reaching high above the rooflines is a viridian green cupola, glinting in the morning sun. Drawing the eye as fiercely as any dome, its celestial curves beckon the traveller forward – and it is to this shrine that our steps must press. All these other buildings, of bricks and walls and bolted doors; all this readiness of barricades and ball, of guns and powder designed to defend against an invader from without, are nothing compared to the attack from within. It is this latter that is the sternest test – all the rest, as my mother might have said, is 'small potatoes'.

Stepping inside, I closed the door gently and the cacophony of the outer world, of cars and naval guns, of calls and cries and whirring helicopters, faded to a distance. I became enveloped by a concentrated self-awareness. The ceiling is high, the walls are bare, the acoustic flat, but the sunlight streaming through the tall windows emphasizes my own, tied nature. Moving from the antechamber, I walk forward through an inner doorway – and stop, for there, in the glory of an eastern light, in the high spaces of a mountain top, is the very echo of the scene (how long ago I cannot now count) that had formed in the rising steams from my pan of potatoes. But that had occurred in Chichester, in the security of a house, whereas here, at the Church of St Michael and All Angels in Paulsgrove, the reality was very different. The details of the depiction were as described, even down to the fists and knots of sandstone cloud and the lumps of rock on the grassy top of the mountain; but so much more was now evident. The figures dominate the scene. Not only that, they dominate the whole church, for the mural is the focal point of the building, a colourful reredos directly behind the altar.

Faced with the reality of the mural, it was apparent that the chosen narrative offered a glimpse of a tantalizing and decisive

Hans Feibusch mural showing the confrontation between Jesus and Satan, St Michael and All Angels, Paulsgrove.

moment in the biblical story: the confrontation between Jesus and Satan at the time (in the account given by St Matthew) of the Third Temptation. From the 'high mountains' the Devil shows Jesus the kingdoms of the whole world and, in hope of a false dream – a commitment to slavery – offers him the kingship. Jesus's reply is devastating in its anger: 'Get thee hence, Satan!' (Matthew 4:10) But that is the way with certainty: there is neither time nor need for the slow, reasoned (so we call it – but it is more often 'self–seeming') process that leads to destruction – spiritually and morally. The act of rejection or assent, when it comes, is decisive in its immediacy (for any dither – shall I, shan't I, join the devil's dance? – is already agreement to a devilish delay) – which is exactly what the muralist's piercing artistry reveals.

Failure in daily living (or even at the last) is a necessary part of what Keats described as the schooling of a soul and, as if in readiness for the final mysteries, there is in this modern church a reminder of that journey of discovery. Painted high on the ceiling, beyond the reach of sublunary mortals, four angels circle the world: three of them gesture heavenwards but the fourth, one arm raised aloft in triumph, the other reaching earthwards in pity, watches over our earthly schooling. And further, as if to emphasize the point, the muralist paints one more lesson. Above the altar, on a pediment high above the Temptation, are depicted the Wise and Foolish Virgins: five with lamps aflame (for they are alert to life's opportunities) light the bridegroom to the marriage feast, while five, their lamps drained dry from an indolent abandon, forfeit the chance to walk with hope and, desolate in emptiness, plead forgiveness.

By whom such a telling conjunction of images was conceived is not recorded in the church, but in bold letters to the lower left of the altarpiece is the name of the muralist: FEIBUSCH 57. Enquiry elicited that this was Hans Feibusch. Born of Jewish parentage in 1898, he had fled Germany in 1933, embraced Christianity in the 1940s and later, with encouragement from George Bell (sometime Bishop of Chichester), decorated in the

1950s and 1960s many Anglican churches with scenes from the Bible. Most of these churches are in London, but in Sussex, as well as two examples of his work in Chichester, there are three others: at Goring-on-Sea (St Mary's), at Brighton (St Wilfrid's) and at Eastbourne (St Elisabeth's). And at Iden, near Rye, there is a painting, *Return of the Prodigal Son*, which was exhibited at the Festival of Britain in 1951.

A marked feature of all these works is the vibrancy of palette. It is a vibrancy associated with a Mediterranean use of colour; but more important is the way a Feibusch mural sings in harmony with the architectural spaces in which he worked. Yet this harmony, of paint with stone, of design with building, is not the only music that can be played by an artist and a building: poets can sing as brightly, and with as much colour and reference too. Listen to

> [these] thousand things:
> The stars of Heaven, and angels' wings,
> Martyrs in a fiery blaze,
> Azure saints mid silver rays,
> Moses' breastplate, and the seven
> Candlesticks John saw in Heaven,
> The winged lion of Saint Mark,
> And the Covenantal Ark –

all of which occur in a poem written more than 150 years ago, the inspiration for which we can visit as we journey from Paulsgrove back to Chichester.

Cross from Hampshire back into Sussex, turn north into Stansted Park and find the chapel. It was there, at a service on 25 January 1819, that the poet John Keats witnessed the dedication of the east window, which was designed by Lewis Way, the then owner of Stansted. Way's mission in life was laudable – 'tolerance to the Jews and their entry into the family of society'. In pursuit of this cause he established at Stansted a Hebrew College, pleaded his cause in Moscow, before Czar Alexander I, and attended the 1818 Congress at

Aix-la-Chapelle, where he was instrumental in securing a clause in the Protocol that accommodated his devotion to Jewish rights.

It was this same devotion that led Way to incorporate in his design for the window the biblical motifs that occur in the lines given above from Keats' poem, 'The Eve of St Mark'. But it was not the east window alone that caught the poet's eyes during the long service. In a draft for another poem, 'The Eve of St Agnes', we are told of a room where

> A casement tripple arch'd and diamanded
> With many coloured glass fronted the Moon
> In midst (w)hereof a shi(e)lded scutcheon shed
> High blushing gules –

Reredos at Stansted Chapel with a Hebrew inscription – Yahweh *(the name of God).*

and that in this room of diamond panes and golden glass (a reference, it is thought, to a window that is no longer extant on the northern side of Stansted Chapel) there 'kneeled saintly down a maiden, who inly prayed [as she waited for her knight-in-arms] for grace and heavenly boon'.

But Madeline, for that was the maiden's name, was the invention of the poet, not of the glass designer, and the boon she sought – the discovery of her own story – was a story she won only in hardship. Her future, a future to be lived in exile from her own, was to be one of storm, of deprivation even, far removed from the 'poppied warmth of sleep' that embraced her after the long vigil. And yet, so urgent was the story she yearned for, so soon as she was roused by her knight, she abandoned – without the hint of a taste – the feast he had prepared of

> candied apple, quince, and plum, and gourd;
> With jellies soother than the creamy curd,
> And lucent syrops tinct with cinnamon;
> Manna and dates in argosy transferr'd
> From Fez; and spiced dainties, every one,
> From silken Samarcand to cedar'd Lebanon.

But enough! there must be a stop: this is more than heart and tongue can bear. And in any case, it is time to return to Chichester or that plate of potato will grow whiskers.

Alas, the earthy produce from my flint-strewn ground is no rival to the sumptuous riches of Samarcand; no argosy breasts the salty seas with destined fruits and mystic spice for my eager table. The plate is cold, the potatoes black and the oil (ugh!) has gone rancid. To hell with the devil's work. Next year I shall grow strawberries . . . learn to blow glass . . . and, with a steady hand, cast them in globes of crimson light.

REVISITING A PLEASURE SPOT: DAY-TRIP TO BUTLINS, SOUTHCOAST WORLD

Jan Ainsley

I do not travel anywhere lightly. On this particular journey on the 7.15 a.m. from London Victoria to Southcoast World, Bognor Regis, I felt especially laden. I was not weighed down by my usual overcrowded suitcases – even I can manage with a small holdall for a day-trip – but I was struggling, with an uneasy mixture of happy memories of childhood holidays spent at camps and a later education that questioned such pleasures. Today I returned to one of my childhood haunts to see what holiday camps, now known as centres, are like in 1995.

Every summer throughout later childhood, Mom, Dad, my sister and I set off in Dad's Austin 35 to drive from Birmingham to a holiday camp just outside Weston-Super-Mare. I was the daughter of a new postwar species, the affluent male manual worker – a species imagined only by keeping a sociological gaze firmly in the bingo position, eyes cast downward in the direction of what was then known as the 'rough' working class. In contrast with the 'rough', my 'respectable' Dad earned high wages during Macmillan's 'never had it so good era', and we proudly displayed our prosperity by holidaying at camps.

My memories of holiday camps are happy ones. Ensconced in our pleasure domes, we were sold a tantalizing package. Everything was provided in those mini-towns for the deserving working class who, from 1938 onwards, had been entitled to enjoy their landmark achievement of an annual week's holiday with pay. Holiday camp advertising promised value for money and no risk of debt. This spirit was captured in Billy Butlin's slogan: 'A week's holiday for a week's pay'.

For us, this was a thrift that purchased luxury. The camp replaced a rented caravan in Weston where mornings had been spent hunting for the seashore when the tide was out. Even now I can recall the relief of jumping into a heated indoor swimming pool instead of cold murky water in which paddling merited a Queen's Guide badge for endurance. Every day I looked forward to eating three big meals in a cavernous dining room. I enjoyed the freedom of wandering around without my parents and stalking my closely chaperoned older sister for sightings of romance. In the evenings I played at being grown up by waltzing with my Dad in glittery chandeliered ballrooms to the music of Mantovani look-alikes. It was so glamorous. I could almost have imagined that I was in Hollywood.

I detected that all was not well with my pleasures when I passed the eleven-plus and was ticked into grammar school. But it was not until some years later, under the civilizing influence of a university education in the social sciences, that I learned more about the significance of holiday camps. They were part of something called the 'masses'.

Amid the many changes signified by the emergence of a modern western world, one important one was the creation of a mass, as in 'mass media', 'mass entertainment' and 'mass culture'. I had never heard my family use that word. Such an omission was not surprising as I had attended lectures which taught me about the supposed 'restricted' language code of the working class. Moreover, it was not a self-ascribed word. You had to be a 'non-mass' in order to recognize one. Evidently, holiday camps overflowed with meaning, especially about the masses: camps were associated with semi-detached houses, commercial television, Woolworth's, drip-dry shirts and Hollywood movies. If asked, I could have written an essay on all of these.

Fortunately, I was not alone in the embarrassment engendered by my life outside university. Welfare State Britain had thrown up other similarly dislocated individuals whose academic success created a disturbing homelessness. During term-time I sheltered with other vulnerable working-class students floundering in this wilderness of 'upward social mobility'. Overwhelmed by the promise of gain and blinded to any loss, we compliantly shook off the vulgarity, tastelessness and cultural deprivation of our extra-university lives.

Until today, I had not been to a holiday camp in thirty years. Despite the education, I still felt a *frisson* of pleasure at the thought of returning. But with my childhood memories and subsequently acquired intellectualized gaze, what would I see now?

The train arrived on time at Bognor Regis. Judging by the number of fellow travellers catapulted by bulging suitcases onto the platform across the vertiginous chasm which divides British Rail trains from their platforms, quite a few of us were heading for Butlins. Since 1960, Butlins has marked the boundary between Bognor Regis to the west and Felpham to the east, and many town dwellers consider the arrival of Butlins to have marked the end of any aspiration to attract a nice class of visitor, perceiving 'Butlin Regis' as change but not improvement.

I joined the other exiles from normal life as they listed along the platform to the pick-up point. Ten minutes later we were deposited at the main entrance. As I was not a proper holiday-maker, I had to circle around to the other side of the camp to the entrance for day visitors, and I followed the high perimeter fence which encloses Butlins. Each vertical bar concludes with a Neptune topping, which curiously gives an impression of curving inwards as if designed around the impossibility of escape rather than the security of enclosure. As I walked past the chalets, a quiet voice from somewhere behind the fence confirmed the clichéd suspicion of camps as prisons: 'Can we have our ball back please?' I retrieved the ball and threw it back in the vague direction of four lads, united by a premature middle-aged spread and glowing Arsenal shirts.

The fixed smile of the attendant taking my entrance money reminded me of a key component of the holiday camp formula: the cornucopia of delights are packaged around having fun and being seen to have fun. Mr Happiness, as avuncular Sir Billy

The iron perimeter fence: Southcoast World, Bognor Regis.

Butlin was known, may not have read Freud, but he knew all about the pleasure principle. There is an invisible sign over the entrance that reads: 'You are now entering an angst-free zone. Leave all your emotional baggage at reception.' In the short distance from the entrance, across a car park which contained no ugly Volvos, into the heart of Pleasureville, I met six staff oozing cheerfulness. Judging by the ache in my cheek muscles, I thought I was holding my own on the smile count. But the 'cheer up it might never happen' from one of the passing 'angels' in red polyester uniform suggested otherwise, and I headed off in pursuit of the nearest video monitor to practise smiling.

Feeling somewhat reassured, I set off for the crossroads on the long concrete highway known as Main Street. Buildings in all sorts of colours, materials, shapes and sizes rise up on either side. Regency style doors and windows, Tudor timbering and multicoloured plastic cladding all suggest a heterogeneity reminiscent of many towns in modern Britain but not reminiscent of my childhood holidays. Uniformity has been abandoned in a display of choice. This is most visibly symbolized by the architectural nuances which mark off the three-tiered accommodation. In my day we were all one class.

The cluster of shops on Main Street is dubiously advertised as exclusive on the Channel Five monitor. Whoever made the claim skilfully illustrates that familiar admaker strategy of working with the masking rather than the revelatory power of words. Window shopping was as enticing as wrestling with Borneo Bill, who was scheduled to appear that night at one of the 'hot spots'. I did not buy anything and, according to one shop assistant, I was not alone. She struggled unsuccessfully to remember her last sale.

Pretty Things, with teddy bear logo and pink canopy, stocked plenty of nylon nets and ruched blinds to decorate your home. They were a rather different souvenir to the ones my Mom used to purchase: she always bought china donkeys and other assorted trinkets designed to remind you of the pleasures of holidays and to let all the neighbours know where you had been for your holidays. Opposite, Sticky Choice is dedicated to selling anything whose primary ingredient is sugar. It is situated immediately next door to the gym. Further along, Everydays, complete with pastel pink and lemon candy stripe awning, delivered its promise of convenience foods. Also on Main Street are a smattering of fair stalls of the old-fashioned throw-a-coconut variety and a clothes stall promising a unique 'just for you' designed T-shirt. Everywhere I looked there was no shortage of opportunities to spend your money. As I stood at the crossroads I spotted a familiar sight: Quicksilver, the amusement arcade.

The arcade was dark. The solitary figures standing in front of the machines played with a concentrated but hopeful seriousness. On most of the gaming machines the potential pot of gold is not on a Las Vegas scale, but the £50 won by the woman next to me delighted her. She rushed off to spread the news of the good luck which equalled her weekly wage.

I did not last long in Quicksilver. The noise of the machines and rave music was deafening. I like loud music but I am puzzled why amusement arcades full of noisy machines find it necessary to play loud music, unless it is to deaden your short-term memory into forgetting how much money you had prior to gambling. Looking out from the doorway onto a bright sunlit Main Street, my attention was caught by a drift of buggies heading into the Plaza. Could this be lunchtime?

The Plaza is one of several buildings at Butlins where it is difficult to work out the relationship between exterior structure and interior function. It is housed inside one of those giant recycled hangars which are an architectural hallmark of Butlins, downmarket supermarkets and do-it-yourself emporia. Three of its exterior walls are made of solid blue plastic sheeting. Given the desired illusion of outdoor eating but the vagaries of English weather, the fourth wall is all glass. Once inside, this al fresco illusion is sustained by roof lighting which mimics the illumination of the sun and by flooring designed to imitate piazza brick.

All around the sides of the hangar are situated the various food dispensaries. The flavour is international: English (roast chicken, baked potatoes); French (pancakes); and Italian (pizza). In my day it was 'meat and two veg' twice a day. Although there is now more variety, eating lots frequently remains an important item in the Butlins formula.

Everyone was eating at the chairs and tables placed between the food dispensaries and the architectural centrepiece: a Moorish bar, which rises Phoenix-like to the hangar roof. Its structure has a thick, iced-cake fascia. Reminiscent of old Hollywood film sets, the illusion of a first floor inside the bar is created by windows which have no interior room into which to cast light and no staircase permitting access. Scattered round the bar is a small selection of large plastic trees complete with peeling plastic bark revealing a black plastic spine. Two of the trees are draped with flashing Christmas lights, most of which have lost the knack of flashing.

After eating my French pancake, I set off for Rainbow Oasis, the unheated outdoor children's pool, the full-time residents of which are plastic dolphins and rhinos which could be seen as kitsch in a more fashionable setting. The blue-lined pool is surrounded by a flat expanse of concrete. Grass is in short supply throughout the camp. Scattered over the concrete is an abundance of wooden picnic tables with inseparable benches. A few metres away, lorries rumbled by on the main road. Initially the noise suggested that the location of the pool jarred with the holiday promise of 'getting away from it all'. But perhaps such glimpses of the 'real world' are a useful reminder to the holiday-maker of where else they could be.

Today the spell of Mediterranean weather made for a crowded pool and familiar pleasures, even down to the anxious skyward looks checking for an early warning of approaching clouds. The heat had done little to raise the temperature of the water and my toes were tentatively stuck into it prior to any commitment to further immersion. This was an aspect of my holidays that I had erased from my memory.

Around the pool, people were busy reading large paperbacks and popular newspapers, acquiring suntans, eating, drinking, talking and, most noticeably, smoking. Even more noticeable was that the smoking was brazen and unashamed. The widespread scattering of stubs bore witness to the continuation of an addiction which no longer shelters under the protective wing of a liberal embrace. When I was a child everyone smoked. I furtively experienced my first packet of five untipped Woodbines when left alone in a holiday chalet. Movies and advertisements created potent equations: money, love, desirability and nicotine. This must be one of the few public places left where the transformation of the smoker from hero to outcast has not taken place.

Holiday camps are also some of those rare places in England where children are welcome. Here kids can disappear into Wizzy's World, go to discos and the fair, ride donkeys and go-carts, and join in any number of other activities. There were children of all ages in and around the pool. Many were very recent arrivals in this world. Toddlers bounced and lurched around. Youngsters played games with Dads, including some who looked rather unpractised at parenthood. Fashionably dressed teenagers wandered around, sometimes sitting with their parents, sometimes huddled in giggling groups away from immediate parental surveillance. Curiously, the most noticeable teenagers were not the ones on holiday but the ones who worked there. The young workers were distinguishable from the holiday-makers by their uniform of yellow and orange T-shirt and shorts. Judging by their exotic accents, these were the sort of New Age travellers who would have the government stamp of approval.

Bodies scattered in and around the pool were marked off from each other in many ways, not just by clothes and age. All skin colours were there – the shades of blue of the recently arrived Geordies, a widespread scatter of winter-whitened, the golden tanned, and the deep black of the family sitting next to me. Extremes of metabolism were everywhere. I felt cheered to see so many seemingly unselfconscious women obliged to overflow from swimming costumes which are always made from stretchy material capable of containing only the slightest of flesh. Were they immune to the potent tyrannical illusion that slimness is the necessary precondition for the attainment of that elusive trinity: beauty, love and happiness?

Wanting to find the heated indoor swimming pool of my childhood, I headed off to find Aquasplash. Nowadays pools are called complexes, the only legitimate complex permitted on a holiday camp. This one boasts of being the largest in Europe. On the outside its opaque, blue, stretched skin finishes in an atrium roof. Its intestine-like tunnels of fun are displayed on the outside. Inside, even on a hot day like this, there were plenty of people. The water is kept at a constant temperature in pools which gesture towards exotic tropical locations in the form of plastic palm trees. The loud buzzer warned of the start of the wave machine, an innovation since my childhood. I naïvely thought that wave machines served the purpose of improving swimming skills in a simulated sea. I soon realized that their illusion is the rather more appealing one of activity in passivity. All that swirling round took place regardless of effort. Altogether, little swimming occurs at Aquasplash. It is too full of other attractions such as slides and shoots and safe paddling areas. For someone who loathes sport, I left feeling rather virtuous – and decided it was time to head home.

Long after I reached home, I found myself still at Butlins struggling to know what I had seen. Who was this 'I' who had been hanging about watching and listening? Was it the naïve child 'I' hearing whispers of idealized memories? Was it the guilty student 'I' who had joined in the chorus of condemnation of my family's pleasures? Was it a more dissenting middle-aged 'I' who fluctuates between denigration and celebration of popular pastimes? All these 'I's, and a few unspoken ones, swirled around in kaleidoscopic fashion. Was that peeling paint on windowsills tatty or did it reveal an interesting patina? Was all that plastic naff or a robust refusal of romance? Did I see minnows shepherded around from one pleasure spot to another or discerning people deciding on their day? The belief in the existence of a mass of the dangerous, mindless or tasteless variety, and the resistance such beliefs generate, has so framed my vision that I cannot lay claim to an innocent gaze. I had kidded myself that the purpose of this day-trip was to check out some memories. Partly this was true, but partly I wanted to be able to defend the popular pleasures of 'ordinary' people.

Despite the attempt to stay ahead of its sell-by date signalled by the change of name from Butlins to Southcoast World, the cornucopia seemed rather tame, dull and expensive. It justifies itself in the same way as all those critics I still read: 'We know them better than they know themselves.' Translated into a mass consumer industry, that becomes known as: 'We give 'em what they want.' After all, they wouldn't be there if they didn't want to be, would they?

Yet could it be that the punters are less fooled than the critics and the providers. Throughout the day I eavesdropped on people messing about, having a laugh, having a drink, getting irritated with each other and having a moan about the place. I even detected irony. As the cliché claims, appearances can be deceptive. The inner world of people's thoughts are not waiting to be read just because they go to Butlins, any more than voting habits are revealed by purchasing the *Sun* newspaper. But masses will always be crowds denied the subtleties and nuances which characterize the life and feelings of the non-mass.

The attractions of Butlins are not a mystery. There is a security in its familiarity. It is reassuring to recognize the logos, the language and the entertainment. Many people living precariously for fifty-one weeks of the year are unlikely to hunt out exciting adventures in those exotic strange places which are the holiday locations of the affluent and the travel writer. With one or two weeks at most, time is precious. The absence of guidebooks and the presence of organized entertainment is a bonus. Moreover, camps offer women that which for so long was a male preserve, the possibility of going on holiday and actually having one. For parents the supervised childcare enables them to square the circle and be good parents while not spending every moment in each other's company.

Is to go there to be duped? Are they duped any more than I was on my 'real' summer holiday in my French farmhouse? That, too, was packaged, and around exactly the same heady myths of sun, romance and, that most potent illusion of all, escapism.

COMING INTO SUSSEX

Leslie Norris

I came into Sussex in 1955, although I had for years been aware of the county. I had a friend, an old clergyman who lived in Herstmonceux, an admirer of smooth-haired fox terriers as I was, and our correspondence had alerted me to Sussex. When I thought of becoming a headmaster, the south land was in my mind.

But I am a Welshman. There were posts in Shropshire and Herefordshire that were attractive and closer to home. I didn't really consider moving from Bath, the gracious and comfortable city in which I was living, down to the south coast. In the event I was invited to visit two schools, one in Shrewsbury, which I knew I would take if it were offered to me, the other in Aldingbourne, an unknown village between Chichester and Arundel. I went first to Aldingbourne, as much for the experience as anything else.

Chichester was a revelation. I stayed in North Street and walked about the city. I knew about Keats and his visit to Chichester. I walked through Priory Park to the Guildhall where Blake was acquitted of the crime of treason. It seemed to me I was home. The next day I went to Aldingbourne School – which confused me by being not in Aldingbourne but in Westergate – spoke to the committee, accepted the headship, and telephoned to Shrewsbury to say I would not be attending their interview.

I still don't understand why this happened. Westergate is not a pretty village. It wasn't then and is even less picturesque now. It is a long, straggling street on the A29, a few miles north of Bognor Regis. It is as flat as a table. To the south of the village the railway runs east–west, the rails lifted perhaps a foot above the ordinary surface of the road, an eminence which allows the natives to call the level-crossing Mount Woodgate. The village houses are a miscellaneous lot, few of them having any character at all. Here and there an old thatched cottage suggests there might be more to the place than meets the eye. And indeed there is.

When my wife and I walked into School House, we were confounded by the chaos of our furniture, piled haphazardly in our absence. We had, almost before we could gasp, a visitor. He was our neighbour, Mr Digance. He offered his assistance in putting our chairs and beds and chests where they should be. He was, he said, an expert in such things. I looked at him dubiously. Small, smiling, middle-aged, he seemed an unlikely expert. But without any fuss at all, he carried even our most heavy pieces to their appointed places, by some sort of persuasion almost. And he didn't stop talking. Among other things, he was the village historian. He possessed the only authentic text of the Mummers' Play, a version unique to the village, and which he had produced many times. He talked to us about a village which we had not seen, indeed was not really visible.

'We didn't used to live here,' he said. 'We used to live around by the church.'

'Did you?' I said stupidly. 'You moved to a bigger house, I expect.' He put down the chair he was carrying, a dining chair, one of six which had belonged to my mother. I still have them.

'No,' he said, 'I can't say that. We all moved. The whole village. Lock, stock and barrel.'

We were nonplussed. We had got up very early that morning and travelled down from Bath. We could not understand him.

'Those of us,' said Mr Digance smugly, 'who were still alive.'

'What do you mean?' I said, preparing myself for some terror, perhaps some wartime tragedy of which I was unaware.

'We moved,' said Digance, with patience, as if to an idiot, 'because of the Black Death. We all lived near the church; then when the Black Death came to the village, we moved out here. Decimated us, it did.'

'Oh, it would have,' I said. 'But that was centuries ago.'

'Exactly,' Mr Digance said, 'and that's why we live in Westergate and not Aldingbourne. Westergate is a new village.

Compared, that is.' He looked with satisfaction around our orderly house. 'Welcome to Westergate,' he said. 'You can still see the mounds of the old houses, if you fly over. As well as the mound of the cathedral. The one we built before they took it all into Chichester.' And he left.

In the morning we found a bunch of spring flowers on our doorstep. We had been formally welcomed.

In those days we had no streetlights in Westergate. The village council fought as one man against such innovations. Perhaps they all shared Mr Digance's vision of the medieval existence of the place; perhaps, as they argued, such illumination would only encourage motorists, strangers most of them from Boxgrove or Barnham, to race even faster down the Street, as our single thoroughfare is named, or perhaps the introduction of lights would turn our innocent young into cynical counterparts of the youth of Bognor. Even so, if I had to go out on winter evenings, the darkness was enough to make me cautious, tentative about even the step outside my own front door. Far away, pale as the furthest star, one useless light shone above the door of The Prince of Wales (and what was he doing here?). At the other end of the village and quite out of sight, a similar light suggested that the Labour in Vain was open. It became second nature to pick up a torch every time we went outdoors, to keep spare batteries nearby, to store brown paper packets of candles in a kitchen drawer.

But the springs were heavenly. Old Bill Norris, who was chairman of pretty nearly every committee in the village, brought my wife posies of primroses to celebrate her birthday. They appeared in the nooks of hedges, at the side of the cinder path which connected Hook Lane with the Street. Bill Norris lived in Hook Lane. One day in March of 1956 I walked up the cinder path and he was in the tiny pasture he used to rear his calves – he always had two calves, 'to bring on' – and when he saw me he raised his arms to the sky and shouted: 'Smell the spring! The winter's gone!' And you could smell it, feel the new warmth entering your body, as warm as fresh milk.

184

Bill Norris had been born in the village, all his life faithful to its church, sang in the choir for more than seventy years. He was the personification of old Sussex, big, red-faced, the keeper of tradition. His voice was the loudest and most influential in keeping the winter village in nightly darkness; he knew the local families for generations.

Of one old man, he said: 'There goes Nat, a-staggering along. His father walked just the same, a-staggering. Best man I ever see with a catapult, was his father. Walks through the farmer's fields, about the Major's woods, ping with his catapult, down goes a bird, a pheasant most like. No noise. Under his coat with the bird. Fed his ten children like kings, did Nat's father.'

'How old is Nat?' I said. 'He must be pretty old.'

Bill stared disapprovingly into the distance.

'You got no call to say Nat is old,' he said. 'He's two years younger than I am, and I ain't saying I'm old. He's eighty-one.'

I walked around Aldingbourne church with Bill, saw the faint outlines of the old murals, touched the incised Maltese cross that recorded the visit of Thomas a'Becket on his way to Canterbury, climbed the squat tower and, looking around, saw the clear lines of the Downs, Halnaker Mill as visible as if I stood just a yard away. We could see Chichester Cathedral. Far off the sea glistened between the Sussex shore and the low hills of the Isle of Wight. I understood that Bill was showing me the important things of his life. It was my initiation. I had become accepted, a Sussex native.

So I built a house, in the half acre which had been the village pond. During the First World War so many horses had been kept there, rounded up for the army, that they had rebelled, broken down the flint wall and escaped into the village. It was still possible to determine where the wall had been repaired, lovingly, by some craftsman still able to build with flints. The wall is a treasure, on the register of protected buildings, although nowadays heavy and continuous traffic shakes it, and I fear for it. My mother came to stay with us, never failing, when she returned on the bus from Chichester, to direct the driver to stop at the Love's Labours Lost, so renaming the more humble Labour in Vain.

My study used to house the electricity generators that lit the village. Bill Norris and his cronies are long dead and the village is brightly lit. After forty years I have left the village, gone out of Sussex.

I have sold my house, something I found almost unbearably hard, and live thousands of miles away. Yet I still know pretty well every stone and blade of grass, if not every house, in Westergate. I could take you along the footpaths that lie under the houses newly built on them. I know where the mallard had their nests. I can hear village voices more clearly than the television news that informs me of current wars and celebrations. I remember the click of snooker balls in the men's club. When last I walked in Westergate there were places I did not know. We used to live there, but we moved away, 'cobweb, leaf and lily'.

BIBLIOGRAPHY

This bibliography includes, in a single alphabetical listing, two kinds of item: firstly, volumes that provide background sources for the themes that figure in several of the contributions and, secondly, other works by some of the present writers. The listing is not exhaustive. Place of publication is given only if outside London.

Admiralty Chart 2045, *South Coast – Outer Approaches to the Solent*, Taunton, Hydrographics Office, 1974

Belloc, Hilaire. *The Cruise of the 'Nona'*, Constable, 1925

——. 'The South Country' in *The Four Men: A Farrago*, London, Nelson and Son, 1912

Bessborough, Earl of. *A Place in the Forest: Being the Story of Stansted in Sussex*, Batsford, 1958

Burton, John F. and Davis, John. *Downland Wildlife: A Naturalist's Year in the North and South Downs*, George Philip, 1992

Chilcott, Tim. *A Real World & Doubting Mind: A Critical Study of the Poetry of John Clare*, Hull, Hull University Press, 1985

Ellman, Richard. *Oscar Wilde*, Hamish Hamilton, 1987

Feaver, Vicki. *The Handless Maiden*, Jonathan Cape, 1994

Fish, Stanley. *Doing What Comes Naturally*, Oxford, Clarendon Press, 1989

Foster, James. 'Charlotte Smith: Pre–Romantic Novelist' in *Proceedings of the Modern Languages Association*, Volume 18 (1928), pp. 463–75

Foster, Paul. *Gilbert White and his Records: A Scientific Biography*, Christopher Helm, 1988.

—— (ed.). *Feibusch Murals: Chichester and Beyond*, Otter Memorial Paper Number 8, Chichester, Chichester Institute, (forthcoming – in press, 1996)

Garland, Patrick (ed.). *Angels in the Sussex Air: An Anthology of Sussex Poets*, Sinclair-Stevenson, 1995

Gittings, Robert. *The Living Year: 21 September 1818– 21 September 1819*, Heinemann, 1954

Grainger, Margaret. 'Some Literary References: Charlotte Smith and Gilbert White' in *The Nightjar: Yesterday and Today*, Otter Memorial Paper Number 3, Chichester, Bishop Otter Trustees, 1988

Hawking, Stephen W. *A Brief History of Time*, London, Bantam Books, 1988

Hilbish, Florence. *Charlotte Smith, Poet and Novelist (1749–1806)*, Philadelphia, USA, 1941

Hobbs, Mary (ed.). *Chichester Cathedral: An Historical Survey*, Chichester, Phillimore, 1994

Hoggart, R. *The Uses of Literacy: Aspects of Working-Class Life*, Chatto and Windus, 1957

Jefferson Airplane. 'When the Earth Moves Again' on *Thirty Seconds Over Winterland*, San Francisco, Grunt Records, 1976

Jones, Barbara. *Follies and Grottoes*, Constable, 1975

Kennedy, Michael. *Portrait of Elgar*, Oxford, Oxford University Press, 1968

Leaska, Mitchell A. (ed.). *A Passionate Apprentice: The Early Journals of Virginia Woolf (1897–1909)*, Hogarth Press, 1990

MacDonald, George. *Twelve of the Spiritual Songs of Novalis*, Arundel, Mitchell and Son, 1851

——. *Annals of a Quiet Neighbourhood*, Hurst and Blackett, 1867

——. *The Princess and the Goblin*, Blackie and Son [1872] 1900

MacDonald, Greville M. *George MacDonald and his Wife*, George Allen and Unwin, 1924

Mackenzie, Murdoch. *Survey by Lieutenant Murdoch Mackenzie of Owers, Chichester and Emsworth Harbours*, Taunton, Hydrographics Office, 1776

MacLeod, Alison. *The Changeling*, Macmillan, 1996

McKillop, Alan. 'Charlotte Smith's Letters' in *Huntingdon Library Quarterly*, Volume 15 (1952), pp. 237–55

McNeillie, Andrew. *The Essays of Virginia Woolf: Volume 1 (1904–1912)*, Hogarth Press, 1986

——. *The Essays of Virginia Woolf: Volume III (1919–1924)*, Hogarth Press, 1988

Mee, Arthur. *Sussex: the Garden by the Sea*, Hodder and Stoughton, 1937

Nicholson, Norman [the geological poet]. *The Pot Geranium*, Faber and Faber, 1954

Norris, Leslie. *Selected Poems*, Mid Glamorgan, Poetry Wales Press, 1986

——. 'The Seeing Eye' in *The Girl from Cardigan*, Mid Glamorgan, Seren Books, 1988

Payne, Shaun (compiler). *A Sussex Christmas*, Stroud, Alan Sutton, 1990

Pevsner, Nikolas, and Lloyd, David. *The Buildings of England: Hampshire and the Isle of Wight*, Harmondsworth, Penguin, 1962

[Plomer, William]. *The Autobiography of William Plomer, with a Postscript by Simon Nowell-Smith*, Jonathan Cape, 1975

Prinzhorn, Hans, *The Artistry of the Mentally Ill*, trans. Eric von Brockdorff, New York, Springer-Verlag, 1972

Pynchon, Thomas. *Gravity's Rainbow*, Jonathan Cape, 1973

Saki. 'Dusk' in *The Complete Works of Saki*, Bodley Head, 1980

Salaman, Redcliffe, N., *The History and Social Influence of the Potato*, Cambridge, Cambridge University Press, 1949

Salkeld, Duncan. *Madness and Drama in the Age of Shakespeare*, Manchester, Manchester University Press, 1994

Schulkind, Jeanne (ed.). *Moments of Being*, Hogarth Press, 1985

Shields, Rob. *Places on the Margin: Alternative Geographies of Modernity*, Routledge, 1991

Shippam Advertising Archive (1900–70), Chichester District Museum, Chichester

Simpson, Jacqueline. *The Folklore of Sussex*, Batsford, 1973

Smith, Charlotte. *Elegiac Sonnets, and Other Essays*, Chichester, 1784 (8th edition, London, 1797)

——. *Beachy Head; with Other Poems*, 1807

Stone, E. Herbert. *The Stones of Stonehenge*, Robert Scott, 1924

Urry, John. *The Tourist Gaze: Leisure and Travel in Contemporary Societies*, New York, Sage, 1990

Walker, Ted. *Hands at a Live Fire: Selected Poems*, Secker & Warburg, 1987

——. *The Last of England*, Jonathan Cape, 1992

Warburton, Nick. *Ackford's Monster*, Walker Books, 1996

——. *Distracted Globe*, Samuel French, 1994

Watson, Lyall. *Dreams of Dragons*, Sevenoaks, Sceptre, 1987

Whitlock, Ralph. *In Search of Lost Gods*, Phaidon, 1979

Williams, Val. *The Other Observers: Women Photographers in Britain 1900 to the Present*, Virago, 1986

Worthing Gazette, and *Worthing Herald*, August and September, 1937, West Sussex County Library, Worthing

Wyatt, John. *Wordsworth and the Geologists*, Cambridge, Cambridge University Press, 1995

Zytaruk, George J. and Boulton, James T. (eds). *The Letters of D.H. Lawrence, Volume II (1913–16)*, Cambridge, Cambridge University Press, 1981